T0209464

Spirit First

Eliezer A. Ramos

WESTBOW
PRESS®
A DIVISION OF THOMAS NELSON
& ZONDERVAN

This book is a work of non-fiction. Unless otherwise noted, the author and the publisher make no explicit guarantees as to the accuracy of the information contained in this book and in some cases, names of people and places have been altered to protect their privacy.

WestBow Press books may be ordered through booksellers or by contacting:

WestBow Press
A Division of Thomas Nelson & Zondervan
1663 Liberty Drive
Bloomington, IN 47403
www.westbowpress.com
1 (866) 928-1240

Because of the dynamic nature of the Internet, any web addresses or links contained in this book may have changed since publication and may no longer be valid. The views expressed in this work are solely those of the author and do not necessarily reflect the views of the publisher, and the publisher hereby disclaims any responsibility for them.

Any people depicted in stock imagery provided by Getty Images are models, and such images are being used for illustrative purposes only. Certain stock imagery © Getty Images.

Scripture marked (MEV) taken from the Modern English Version. Copyright © 2014 by Military Bible Association. Used by permission. All rights reserved.

ISBN: 978-1-9736-7145-9 (sc)
ISBN: 978-1-9736-7146-6 (hc)
ISBN: 978-1-9736-7144-2 (e)

Library of Congress Control Number: 2019911430

Print information available on the last page.

WestBow Press rev. date: 08/14/2019

Dedication

I would like to dedicate this book to my daughter Gabriella. At ten years old, you are one of the most Spirit-led people I know, even when you don't realize it. You have given me nuggets of wisdom that could have only come from the mouth of God Himself, and to this day they still ring true and encouraging in my heart. I pray this book proves that no matter what you feel your weaknesses are, you can do anything as long as you put your mind to it and lean on God for guidance and support. It's my greatest desire that my most memorable accomplishments serve as a launching pad for you to walk into yours, and that my ceiling becomes your floor. You are called to do amazing and wonderful things for the advancement of God's glorious kingdom, and the proof of that is evident in who you are already. You're beautiful, strong, and smart, and you have the most amazing ear to hear God's voice. There's no doubt in me that you will always trust in it. I am a very proud dad and can't wait to see what God does in and through you the more you step into the call that's over your life.

What are you? And what will you always be? I love you!

Goal of This Book

Spirit First is designed to bring an awareness to not only Christians but to every man, woman, and child. Exposing the enemy and his schemes gives people the upper hand to recognize the devil's tactics and be victorious over them. The devil wants nothing more than for people to not understand who God has originally created them to be: a spirit-first human being intimately and spiritually connected to the Creator of the universe. If the father of lies can draw your focus and understanding away from that simple truth, then he's already won. By bringing to light the truths found in this book, those truths can be used as a tool to claim what Jesus has already purchased on the cross and what is already rightfully yours.

God desires to have a spirit-first relationship with every person, just like He had in the garden with Adam and Eve. However, the truth is the world, and even the Church, has wandered so far away from that idea, and now the thought of a spirit-first relationship seems odd. People have become so accustomed to listening to what their flesh says is good that good things seem bad, and bad things seem good. What Jesus came to turn right side up has been flipped upside down yet again. This is the pattern we see throughout the entire Old Testament, and it's continuing into our modern-day New Testament. But God was, is, and always will be faithful, and He has always sent a person or a remnant to call His children home so that they can turn and face the correct way. For Israel it was the judges and the prophets, and for today's sons and daughters, it's whoever will say, "Yes! Send me. I'll go!" Every believer was given exactly what he or she needed at his or her moment of conversion. The only question now is will you use it?

Contents

Introduction

> In the beginning was the Word, and the Word was
> with God, and the Word was God. He was in the
> beginning with God.... And that Word became
> flesh and dwelt among us.   —John 1:1–2, 14

If Jesus Christ is the Word, and the author of Hebrews tells us that
"Jesus Christ is the same yesterday, today and forever," then it is
absolutely safe to say that the Word of God is the same yesterday,
today, and forever as well because they are the same thing. And
if the Word of God never changes, then everything we read is
applicable in this present moment the same as it was yesterday,
and it will be tomorrow. That means what we read in Genesis has a
tie to what we read in Revelation and everything in between. Every
story, every example, every person, and every command has been
placed outside the created order of time, with God, and is then
pulled into time when we apply it to today. This is what John meant
when he said that the Lamb was slain from the foundation of the
world, although it happened thousands of years after creation.
This miracle transcends time yet is applied every time people turn
their hearts to Jesus. It's the same principle applied to the beauty
of a testimony and how the spoken word of a person causes that
very same grace to enter the room and allows all who hear it to
step into its wonder-working power as if it's happening at that
very moment. This is why we overcome Satan and his schemes by

the blood of the Lamb and by the word of our testimony. These things happened in the past, but they are also happening now and forever. If they prove that time knows no bounds when it comes to kingdom principles, then what else throughout the Bible breaks the laws of time and helps us to be conquerors over the enemy and his tactics? The answer is simple: everything we read!

The Christian life is rooted in faith. But faith is never blind, and God has never expected you to free-fall without first giving you a parachute. God will always give us something on which to base our decisions. In the Old Testament, the priests had the Urim and the Thummim to help determine the will of God. In the New Testament, Peter walked with Jesus for years and trusted Him with his life. This is why when he was asked to walk on water, this stretched his faith; it didn't create it. God will never ask you to do something blindly without first building you to a place of trust with Him. Sure, what God asks of us could be challenging at times and even stretch out understanding, but it's never a blind leap of faith. If He asks you to cross the Jordan and fight the giants, it's only because He proved Himself trustworthy in the wilderness first and knows you have what it takes to be victorious. Joshua and Caleb saw the same enormous walls, and the same giants that made them feel like grasshoppers, but they learned something the other ten didn't while in the wilderness that helped pushed their faith to the next level. God will always give you something to stand upon before He brings you face-to-face with the faith challenging decisions that stand between you and His promises for your life.

This book is not designed to be a walk through the entire Bible, but it's a tool to break off the lies of the enemy over the minds of God's people by exposing where and how he attacks us so we can be restored back to the original purpose that God created man for: to walk with Him in the Spirit just like Adam did in the garden before the serpent slithered his way in and influenced the decision that would change everything.

When you're in a war, you need to know your enemy, and this

in-depth look will give the much-needed insight to recognize, counter, and overcome the enemy's tactics. Each chapter will reveal a new enemy and the God-given strategy on how to overcome it, until every minion is exposed and every man and woman of God has the understanding needed to stand victorious over the evil schemes of darkness. It is the goal of this book to equip and empower the reader so that Jesus Christ can receive the full reward of His suffering not only in eternity but now as well! The road our Savior took to Golgotha wasn't just so we can enter the kingdom of God tomorrow, but so that we can also bring it here today!

Declaration

I declare your eyes and ears to be opened to the prompting and leading of the Holy Spirit. I declare that as you read each page of this book, your heart is softened and the capacity of your mind is expanded. I release revelation and wisdom over you right now. Let knowledge and understanding flow through every part of your being with passion and power. I cancel all distractions, weapons of the enemy, confusion, and doubt. No lie will stop you from understanding every word that you read, and you will finish this book. I speak endurance and consistency over you now! For all those scared of reading, and with a history of reading disorders, I bind all reading problems right now, as well as all nervousness and worry that you won't understand what you read or that things won't make sense. I loosen insight, peace, and a new passion and understanding for reading. May you have clarity and focus in the name of Jesus. I declare that those who read this book will become more and more of the new creations that God has intended them to be, and that their relationship with God will grow deeper and more meaningful. Any plan of the devil to stop the spread and use of this book for the growth of God's people is cancelled right now in the name of Jesus. Everyone who looks for wisdom in this book will find it, and this book will bring freedom to many! It's all for the glory of God, in the name of our Lord Jesus Christ. Amen!

Chapter 1

Old Testament versus New Testament

Before jumping into warfare and enemy tactics, a level of identity must be established. You are a son or daughter of God—a Christian—and you are righteous and holy through the blood of Jesus Christ. These are good fundamental truths, but the reality of who you are stretches much deeper than your basic Sunday school teachings. Make it a foundational truth that is forever etched in your mind and firmly written on your heart: you are a spiritual being first. This is the greatest fundamental truth that you can understand as you read through this book! You have a soul, which includes your mind, will, and emotions. You live in a body, which the Bible describes as a temporary tent, but you *are* a spirit!

You were created to be more connected to the spiritual realm than to the physical realm we live in and have grown so accustomed to. The disconnect that has formed since the fall in the garden has led humans so astray that now the physical side of everything takes precedence over the intended spiritual side. We look for physical, tangible answers to the physical, tangible problems we face, not realizing that the majority of them are spiritual problems that are simply manifesting in our physical bodies. This was never God's intention for His creation or His people!

His Intent

In order to understand God's original design and intention, we must go back to the beginning and see how far people have truly fallen. It all starts with one universe-creating idea and the Creator speaking it into existence with those famous four words: "Let there be light!" And of course, if He spoke it, it was done because His speaking is His doing! The Father spoke the Word, and the Spirit made it happen. In the original Hebrew, Genesis 1 verse 2 reads,

> The earth had come together desolate, worthless and empty: cursed. Darkness and obscurity were throughout the deep waters. And the breath of Elohim fluttered gently on the surface of the two joined pieces.

The word *breath* in Hebrew is *ruach,* and it is most commonly referred to as the Spirit of God or the Holy Spirit. So, the Holy Spirit was gently fluttering over the waters, and like glue, He was joining two realms together. What two realms? The supernatural and the natural, or the spiritual and the physical? This is why when the Holy Spirit comes upon people in the Old Testament, they can do supernatural things. It's also why when Jesus, then the apostles and the disciples, and now all who believe step confidently into unity with the Holy Spirit, we see supernatural results. In the Old Testament, the Holy Spirit would clothe and empower one person at a time. But as it was prophesied by the prophet Joel, the Holy Spirit was poured out on *all* flesh at the day of Pentecost (Acts 2), thus empowering all who would receive and walk in Him. This always has been God's intention: to walk in the Spirit.

What Is the Garden?

We all know the garden is not a literal place, right? The garden is always representative of God's three Ps: His presence, His provision, and His purpose. When Adam was placed inside the garden, he was placed inside these three Ps. When Eve was created out of the rib of Adam, she was created inside the garden and already securely inside the presence, provision, and purpose of Yahweh himself. It was there that they would walk and talk with God in the "cool of the day." But what is the cool of the day? Is it a specific time period? Was it when the sun was at its lowest, just before being hidden by the horizon line of the earth? No! It wasn't a time at all. The original Hebrew translation of Genesis 2:8 doesn't use the words "cool of the day." The actual word used is *ruach*. The Spirit of God! Adam and Eve didn't walk with God at a certain time of day or in a certain location. They walked with God in the ruach. They walked with God in the Spirit. All day, every day, everywhere they went, they walked in the Spirit with God completely unhampered and unseparated from Him. They were in perfect covenant, in perfect relationship, and perfectly fashioned together by love Himself. This was paradise at its pinnacle. But we all know the story: this heaven on earth was short-lived because of the slippery, slithering, doubt-infusing, lies of the serpent. Adam and Eve were removed from that perfect connection and immediately thrown into a life where the physical took supremacy over the spiritual. God's intention for humans was put on hold, and His rest had ended. Since that dreadful day, love has been on a radical course to get us back into His garden.

Results of the Fall

It was always God's intention for people to be Spirit led and totally connected to Him at all times. Adam and Eve were spirit first and then physical. But at the tree, by feeding their flesh, they exchanged their Spirit-led lives for a physically motivated mind-set. They flipped everything upside down, leading to the physical hardships. Adam would work and earn a living by the sweat of his brow, Eve would have increased labor pains, and they would both experience the process of physical death. They had stepped into a life directed by their flesh, and the enemy would take advantage of every second of it he could.

When God cursed the serpent, He told him he would eat dust all the days of his life. In order to understand the main tactics of the enemy, we must see the image that is painted here. When God created Adam, He formed him from dust. Adam's *flesh* was made from dust, and the devil was commanded to eat that dust. This is why the devil attacks us in three flesh-driven, physical areas. The first is the lust of the eyes. Eve looked and saw that it was good for food. Second is the lust of the flesh. It was pleasing to her eyes. And third is the pride of life. This means that it would make her wise. All three areas point to the flesh and explain why the devil has access to us only through the decisions we make with our bodies. Jesus knew this, and He knew that the body follows whatever is in a person's heart. That is why He instructed people to guard their hearts and minds and to not commit sinful things in them: because out of the abundance of your heart, your mouth will speak, and your actions will follow. This is also why Paul deemed it so necessary for believers to have transformed minds. They both knew the tactics of the evil one, and now so do you!

Simply put, everything is geared toward the flesh and includes simple attacks on your mind and your heart. But here Adam and Eve stand, removed from constant spiritual connection with God, in a place where their physical bodies now rank supreme over their spiritual beings. This is the very war being waged inside people every second of every day. That is, until the love of the Father sent the Son to turn everything right side up and give *all* the opportunity to step into the garden once again.

What Is the Old Testament?

The Old Testament was the gospel being walked out physically by Israel. Everything we read is the physical side of the Spirit-led life Jesus enabled us to have in the New Testament. This is why Paul declared that we no longer fight against flesh and blood but against the rulers, against the authorities, against the cosmic powers over this present darkness, and against the spiritual forces of evil in the heavenly places. Our flesh and blood represented the physical warfare Israel once waged before Jesus restored the opportunity to walk fully in the Spirit again. Israel could only look to a time such as this because the sacrifice of bulls and goats could not completely take away sin. Therefore, they were still bound to fight the physical battles we read of in the Old Testament. These same physical enemies are the spiritual enemies we face today. If we can understand the story of Israel and what they faced physically, then we will uncover the general process God intends for every Christian and the enemies we face along the way.

Who Is Israel?

In the book of Exodus, Moses stands before Pharaoh and states that God has named Israel as His son and that God has called Israel out to His holy mountain so they can worship Him freely. It was at Mount Sinai that God's promise to Abraham was manifested and Israel walked into covenant and sonship with Yahweh.

Israel represents the believer, both before and after conversion. When we choose to believe and follow Jesus, the Bible says we become children of God—sons and daughters of the King! These fundamental truths give three significant stories in the New Testament deeper meaning: the baptism of Jesus, the teaching to Nicodemus in John 3, and the promised gift of the Holy Spirit on the day of Pentecost.

If Israel was God's son, then why was Jesus called God's Son during His baptism in the Jordan? In order to wrap your mind around this answer, it's imperative that you first step outside of westernized thinking and into the minds and customs of the Jews at that time. To Jews, the dove didn't represent the Holy Spirit; the dove was their symbol and represented Israel itself. So, upon baptism, the dove was visibly seen to rest upon Jesus, which to Israel signified that Jesus was taking up their mantle. He was walking as though He was Israel himself, and the voice of the Father confirmed that when He declared Him His son. This is why the first place Jesus went after His baptism was the wilderness. Jesus, walking as Israel, would be tempted and stretched in the wilderness just like Israel was on their road to the Promised Land. But where they stumbled and even failed, Jesus would succeed! Whereas Israel complained about food (Numbers 11:1–4), and Adam and Eve ate of the tree, Jesus refused to turn the rocks into bread. When the newly freed Israelites committed sexual sin (1 Corinthians 10:7–8) and the first Adam and his wife couldn't help but look upon the fruit with consuming eyes, Jesus refused to throw His body from the temple. When Israel was oblivious to the truth that they were a royal priesthood and murmured about their status (1 Corinthians 10:9–10) and the first two that were made in the image of God, desired to be God, Jesus stood upon His Father's truth of His sonship, looked out from the top of the highest mountain and rebuked the devil's offer to be something He was already destined to be. Yeshua reclaimed the victory that was once lost in the beginning and in the wilderness!

Now, knowing that Jesus was carrying the mantle of Israel throughout His ministry here on earth, further revelation of John 3 and the teaching of Nicodemus comes to light. Again, it's crucial to step out of the realm of westernized thinking to understand this story in its context as well. The Bible wasn't directly written to modern-day Christians. It can be applied and used by people of any time period, but the stories we read have significant meaning to the people of that time, especially to the Jews. In that era, the most important story to the Jewish people was the story of the Exodus. It holds so much significance because that was when they officially became a people and a chosen nation. This was when they knew themselves to be God's one and only son. When Jesus tells Nicodemus that God gave the world His one and only son, Nicodemus would not picture Jesus; rather, he would picture himself and all of Israel. God so loved the world that He gave the world Israel, that whoever would believe in the God Yahweh that Israel follows and believes in would have everlasting life. Israel's life was meant to be the reflection of God's holy and perfect standard. Yes, we know that the only way to the Father is through Jesus, but Nicodemus didn't know that yet. This was an eye-opening rebuke from the great rabbi that left Nicodemus very aware of not only who Jesus was, but of who he was failing to be. Nicodemus and all of Israel were failing to be the priests they were called to be. God didn't send Israel into the world to condemn and point their fingers at the world, but so that the world can be led to God and saved through them. Nicodemus's eyes were opened, and the man who came to Jesus in the dark at the beginning of the chapter was now leaving in the light as a new follower of Jesus!

Jesus's whole mission was to restore what was lost in the garden! His last task was sending the promised Holy Spirit that Israel was afraid to receive. Acts 2 wasn't the first Pentecost. In Exodus, when the angel of death killed the firstborn sons of Egypt, it was on Passover. Israel was released to take a ten-day journey into the wilderness to Mt. Sinai, where Moses would spend forty days on top of that mountain. All of Israel was beckoned to come up the mountain, but shaking with fear, they only sent Moses. After forty days in the presence of God and ten days in the wilderness, for fifty days total, the mountain was filled with great sounds and winds and lots of fire. Moses descended, glowing with the glory of God.

Fast-forward, and Jesus tells His followers, on the day of Passover, to wait for fifty days in order to receive the gift of the

Holy Spirit. Fifty days later, just like at Mt. Sinai, there is a loud sound and wind and fire, and the original Pentecost is restored, and just like when Moses commanded all who rebelled to be killed, and three thousand fell by the sword, Peter is now coming to grips with the new revelation of his new position in Christ, and he stands up and declares the gospel. Three thousand are brought to life by becoming followers of Jesus. In this last fulfillment of prophecy, the Savior of the world has restored everything, including our chance and the open choice to step back into the garden.

Putting It All Together

Let's set the stage so we can understand and apply the rest of this book to our walk with God and our lives in general. Israel is playing the role as the believer, and in order to better receive this book's revelation, let's place ourselves in the shoes of the Israelites. As we walk through their process with them, from slavery to promise, we can see that Israel's walk to salvation was the physical side of our spiritual walk. In other words, the more we see through the eyes of Israel physically, the more we will connect what is happening to us spiritually.

The story of Israel starts out just like ours. They were a slave to Egypt and Pharaoh, much like we were slaves to sin and the devil. But God, in His unfathomable love, sends a savior. For Israel it was Moses, and for us it was Jesus Christ.

The road to freedom led Israel straight to Mount Sinai, where they stood face-to-face with God as He offered them the opportunity to become His sons and daughters. In other words, this was their altar call, their salvation moment! However, Israel's walk to that holy altar wasn't an easy one. As Pharaoh chased them down, threatening to once again enslave them in the life they so desperately wanted to escape, we see today that for many, the walk to the altar, or the raising of their hand as they accept

Jesus into their hearts, is one of the hardest decisions they'll ever make. Just like Pharaoh, the devil doesn't want you to go free, and he will do whatever he can to keep you in a life of slavery to sin. He will remind you of your past and try and convince you that the only life you knew as a slave, and the things you've done while in it, is the only life you'll ever know. This is his last-ditch effort to keep you from sonship and a covenant that leaves him drowned in the Red Sea!

After Israel establishes covenant at Mt. Sinai and God declares them His son, they're taken into the wilderness, where they're set on a journey to the Promised Land, a land flowing with milk and honey. But what exactly is the Promised Land? Does it really have streams of sweet honey and rivers of creamy flowing milk? Of course not! Then what was Moses really saying as he wrote this description? Let's take a look.

What produces milk? Cows and goats. And what do cows and goats mainly eat? Grass. Now, what produces honey? Bees. And where do bees get the pollen to make the honey? Flowers. So, you have a field of green grass covered in flowers, and where is the most common place you find flowers? In a garden! Moses is telling us that the journey to the Promised Land is really a journey back to the garden and God's presence, provision, and purpose for Israel. But why the wilderness along the way? And what does this mean for us once we accept God's honored position as sons and daughters at His holy mountain, we call the altar? This small passage before entering into God's promise is probably the most defining step in a Christian's walk with God. It was in the wilderness that God became real to Israel. It was there that a God they had only heard about but never experienced became a revealed and loving Father. When they were hungry and thirsty, He was their provider and gave them manna, quail, and water from a rock. When they were sick, He showed himself to be a trustworthy physician who healed all their diseases. Anything and everything Israel needed was given to them. The wilderness is the place where we learn that we can trust God with our lives and that His plans for us are always good. The wilderness is never intended to be a place of wandering and death; it's a place that will teach us everything we need to know so we can be sustained when we reach the Promised Land.

After a sinner's conversion into a saint, God is always looking for ways to reveal Himself, His attributes, and His loving wisdom. This is a continuous process for the rest of a believer's life, but it always leads us to a Jordan River. The Jordan River in the Bible always represents transition. For Elijah, it was a transition into heaven. For Elisha, as he crossed over, it was his move into his calling as a prophet. Naaman didn't have it so easy and was confronted by pride, but he transitioned from his Jordan River experience clean and made new. Jesus was finally released to do what He was sent here to do directly after His feet broke the plain of that same transitional river. However, for Israel, the crossing of the Jordan brought upon a decision that would cost them everything. Every time we learn something different about God, we are taken to a Jordan River moment in our lives. This moment is where we are given the opportunity to take God at His word and transition over into a new level of faith, or to doubt Him, and be sent back into the wilderness to learn what we must have missed. Do we cross, or do we wander? That is the question.

Twelve spies went over. Ten came back discouraged, but two came back filled with determination. All the spies saw the grapes so big that two men had to work together to carry one single cluster. All the spies saw how amazing the land was and that everything God had spoken was true. Those same men who saw the blessings also saw the giants, which made them feel as though they were grasshoppers. Every last one of the twelve stared up at the skyscraping walls of the fortified cities that seemed impenetrable. But why the two different reports when they all saw the same things? Why did ten come back ready to die in the middle of their transition, but two came back excited to finally live after making it? Those same questions can be rephrased and redirected toward Christians today. Why do people settle for manna in the wilderness when they can be eating grapes in the promise? If you find yourself stuck and wandering in the wilderness, ask yourself these simple questions: "What has God taught me that I am not applying? What am I scared of, or what lies am I believing that have kept me out of God's promises for my life?"

It is also important to realize that Israel was still blessed and favored during their time in the wilderness. It is very easy for Christians to fall into deception in the wilderness phase after conversion and stay there all their lives thinking that just because God is providing and showering down favor at times, they are in a good place or that they are even in the will of God for their lives. So, what is the biggest sign that you're stuck in different parts of the wilderness? You find yourself going in circles, facing the same things time after time. Sure, manna will sustain you, but God's intention is not for you to live on the same honeycomb day after day, experiencing the same up-and-down rollercoaster life. His intention is to transition you into a place where you go from glory to glory and live fully in His abundant grace, walking with Him in the Spirit. So many Christians trade their destinies for a life in the wilderness, and some even go back to Egypt. But thank God that Israel's story doesn't end there!

The Promised Land Is Our Garden

Israel eventually made it over the river and into the Promised Land. However, this was only the beginning for them, just like it's only the beginning for the believer. We must not forget that on the other side of our Jordan River of transition is not only God's promises for our life but also the enemies that inhabit that land. All the spies saw the obstacles that stood in their way as they embarked in possessing everything God had planned for them. But remember, only two had faith to actually believe they could have it! Just because you transition into the plans God has for you, that doesn't mean there won't be fierce enemies and towering walls that oppose you. The transition doesn't signify that everything will be easy, but it does reveal that you have what it takes to be victorious! Just like God reminded Joshua, Elohim is reminding you to be strong and courageous and take what He has already declared is yours!

The rest of this book will unmask all the enemies you will face after your moments of transition, as well as the strategies God has given to assure your victory over them. Be strong and courageous as you read on, and know that you already have the victory. All you have to do is apply what you read, allow Holy Spirit to guide you, and then walk in it. By knowing the physical enemies of Israel and what the sons and daughters of God did to defeat them, you will gain the understanding of the spiritual enemies you face and how to apply those same tactics so you too can walk out as a champion and overcomer. As Joshua 1:9 is translated from the original Hebrew, "be a strong, obstinate, hardened conqueror and courageous, alert, strengthened, confirmed, established, fortified and steadfastly minded." Welcome to the Promised Land!

Chapter 2

Knowing Your Enemy

Clearly, our enemy is the devil. But what may come as a surprise to many Christians is that the devil isn't responsible for everything that goes wrong in our lives. Yes, he is the point of origin for evil and sin, and he's the first mastermind behind any and all rebellion, but the truth is he isn't orchestrating everything. He's simply not that strong! So many Christians believe that there is this battle between God and Satan, as if the devil is anywhere near big enough to stand up against the great I Am. The reality is that the counterpart to Lucifer is Michael, not God—and the devil lost that battle too! Christians consistently give the devil too much credit for so many things that go wrong, but the reality is the devil simply isn't that powerful! We live in the world, and humans were given free will. With that free will, we have the option to make choices, and those choices can be bad. With those bad choices, whether intentional or unintentional, we or other people can bear the results. Human beings are the most powerful creations on this planet, and a human being submitted and influenced by the Holy Spirit is unstoppable. But it's important to also know that humans, under the influence of a demonic spirit, can be very powerful as well. This is why the battle for your mind is so imperative and crucial between whether you succeed in reaching your purpose or fail. The devil cannot be two places at once because he is not omnipresent like God is, so he uses other fallen angels, or demons, to carry out tasks and infiltrate people's minds. This is the exact picture of spiritual warfare at its highest.

Let it be brought back to your remembrance that Paul told us in his letter to the Ephesians where demons live and from where they do their warfare: from heavenly places, which the Bible explains are just the skies around the earth, and throughout the universe. Paul also revealed that principalities, powers, and rulers give demons access to our minds. It's by planting lies there, in our thoughts and reasoning, that we, being powerful people, manifest those lies in our actions. The devil and demons have no authority here, so they influence us in many different ways to carry out their evil intentions. It's as simple as a single lie is whispered, a human receives it, and strongholds start to form. In ancient times, a stronghold was known as a secured location with walls and defenses. Spiritually, once a lie is received, a barricade is built around it in your mind and in your heart, and the enemy uses that lie to launch his attack against you and your purpose. One stronghold can branch off into many different areas. For example, a lack of identity will lead to insecurity, insecurity leads to low self-esteem, low self-esteem leads to sexual immorality, sexual immortality leads to rejection, and so on. The root started with a lack of identity and then branched off into many different "sub-strongholds," which could (and usually do) lead to many other broken places. By recognizing the root, we can also eliminate the branches that grow from it. Again, the devil is not anywhere near equivalent to God, so he cannot create like God can. Therefore, the bag of tricks that the thief uses today are the same tricks he worked with in the past against Israel. The only difference is Israel fought the physical battles that we fight in the spirit. The good news is the Bible says that if a thief is found, he must pay back seven times what he stole, even if it means he has to give up everything in his house. As soon as we locate and expose the areas the devil uses to launch his onslaughts against us, we have authority to tell him that the land he's on is no longer his, to stop trespassing, and to put back what he stole sevenfold!

All of the enemies of Israel were living on land that was no longer theirs to inhabit. They were now trespassing on what God had given to his people, and all Israel had to do was take it. Before you gave your heart to the Lord, Genesis 6 tells us, your intentions and motivations were selfish and self-seeking, completely overrun by the evil one. Now, through the purchasing blood of Jesus Christ, we have our land back, and all we have to do is go and take it. But like Israel, we're left with a choice. Will you mount up on wings like eagles and take back what Jesus paid the ultimate price to give you? Or will you cower and live a mediocre life in comparison to what God has planned for you? The choice is yours. It's the power and beauty of free will. If you choose to possess the land the Lord has given to you, here's a look at the enemies you will face.

The Land of Canaan

> When the LORD your God brings you into the land which you are entering to possess and has driven out many nations before you, the Hittites, the Girgashites, the Amorites, the Canaanites, the Perizzites, the Hivites, and the Jebusites, seven nations greater and mightier than you, and when the LORD your God delivers them before you and you strike them down, then you must utterly destroy them totally. You shall make no covenant with them nor show mercy to them. (Deuteronomy 7:1–3)

This is the command of God to Israel as they were about to embark on the greatest quest known in their history, and it is this same command that God is giving to you as you step out in faith and take back what is rightfully yours!

The Canaanites are broken up into two groups. Because they were the dominant faction, the entire land God gave Israel was called the land of Canaan, and therefore all of the people groups are known as Canaanites. This is very important when we start to understand how the Bible describes the Canaanites as a whole, versus the Canaanites as a single people group.

This is a war, and each enemy symbolizes a different battle ground and tactic the enemy uses to influence your mind. When we read that the Canaanites were a large and fierce people and were not easily defeated, we can conclude that this war for control over our minds is not going to be a simple walk in the park. It's going to be met by large and fierce tyrants who do not want to relinquish their footholds. The Israelites were able to overcome the Canaanites and possess the entire land only with divine help. As a matter of fact, whenever they tried to do it on their own, they would fail! That sobering fact opens our eyes and deflates any ego we may start with, and it reminds us that this war is not won in man's strength and wisdom but in God's alone. The Canaanites as a whole were very wicked and idolatrous people. They were known as the people of the lowlands and the plains. This was their reputation physically, and this is where the enemy lays his foundation for all the Canaanite tribes. This means that for Christians, spiritually, many of life's struggles and open doors allowing the enemy access into our minds are centered from within evil and morally wrong choices (wickedness), and strengthened by all the things that raise up a standard over God (idolatry). These are the places the devil and his minions have legal right to build strongholds in a person's life and launch every attack against them. If an idea or action is evil, is selfishly self-seeking, or tries to create a god in the place of God, it's a welcoming open door for an enemy fortress to be built in your mind. These places will create low points and places of spiritual plateaus in your life in general and particularly in your relationship with God.

The first steps to take when tearing down these high and lofty places is to get rid of any pride, redirect your actions and thoughts and attitude toward those of God's, and then remove any idols. An idol is anything that comes before God, whether it's anything that you want with all your heart or it's something you can't stop thinking about. The sneaky trick the enemy will sometimes use on Christians is that these things can be God-given dreams and ideas too. If the dream comes before the One who gives the dream, or the gift is more important than the Gift Giver, and we've fallen into idolatry. Many believers will receive a kingdom-advancing inspiration, love it, invest all their time trying to grow it, and leave nothing left for God, thus accidently creating an idol in its place. This gives the enemy legal right to form a stronghold over that place of favor, and now what God intended to use to bring you closer to Him has led you astray. These wicked and idolatrous places must be removed first so Holy Spirit can be Lord in all areas and bring freedom. Just like Joshua was instructed to not keep one single person, animal, or item from any of these lands, we must not keep one hint of any of these characteristics, or they too will be a constant annoyance, a thorn in our flesh, that rises up against us when we least expect it and causes unnecessary battles for the rest of our lives.

The Canaanites

(Facing the Past)

It is appropriate to start with the Canaanites because they were the strongest and most feared of all the groups in Canaan. Just as they were a physically tough enemy for Israel to face, this battle in the spiritual is always the hardest and most avoided. However, it's important to know that it holds the most influence over the lives of the Christian. The Canaanite walls were towering, their fortifications were extremely impressive, and their people were giants so big that the Bible tells us that Israel said they felt like grasshoppers in comparison to them.

Their name is translated as *humiliation* and *disgrace*, and it was given to them because of where they came from in their past. Ham, Noah's youngest son, had disgraced and humiliated his father, and as a result his son was cursed. The past would undoubtedly follow Canaan, and his people would soon be known for a mistake made in their prior history. Everything with this enemy stemmed back to the past here, and it is the same spiritual root of this battle for Christians today. Unmistakably, the biggest obstacle for today's believers is dealing with humiliation, disgrace, shame, hurts, and choices made in their past! Not only does the enemy take careful consideration in how to build seemingly unmovable walls, but sadly we do as well.

The Canaanite cities were built between Tyre and Gaza, which mean a rock and a strong place, respectively. So, the saying, "a rock and a hard place" can really be about being stuck between your past and your present, or where you've been and where God wants to take you. This is why we find these locations by the edge of the sea and the Jordan River. It's already been established in a previous chapter that the Jordan River signifies transition, and there's no question as to why the first thing we run into when trying to transition into the promises God has for us is our past. With every transition we face to go deeper into where God is taking us, we come up against a constant reminder or an obstacle created in our past that makes us feel small and insignificant. This is the Canaanite stronghold of the enemy: to remind us, try to use our past against us, and keep us running back to "Egypt" in fear. In the reality of these situations, it makes no sense to run from our past or to our past, yet many Christians will resort to the very things that brought them such shame in the first place in order to cope, and as a result they're refortifying the enemy's walls.

So how do we overcome those walls, and face those giants? Israel was warned by Yahweh that if they faced the Canaanites while they were turning away from the Lord, they would fail. The first thing we have to do to claim the victory is focus our eyes on the Author and Finisher of our future and our faith, Jesus Christ! In Numbers 21, the Israelites made a vow to God, dedicating themselves to Him. When you fix your eyes on Jesus, you must also say within yourself that whatever it takes and no matter what rises up against you, you will see this through to the end. Now, the last place the Word of God describes the Canaanites making their dwelling is by the Oak of Moreh. When translated from Hebrew to English, it means *stretching*.

This fight with the shame, hurt, and humiliation of your past will not be a quick and easy battle to be won. It's a process that will cause you lots of spiritual stretching. But if you stay determined, the victory will be given to you! That's right, *given* to you. Israel was instructed to send Judah into the battles against the Canaanites, and *Judah* means *praise*. King David reminds us to bless the Lord at all times and praise His holy name. When the stretching gets tighter, the pull gets stronger, and the thoughts of your past get to be too much, there must be an anthem of praise that rises from within you. The Canaanites feared Israel because of the testimony of miracles that God performed for them in the wilderness. Those times of learning and understanding God more were not just to get you into the Promised Land; they were so that you will have a praise in your mouth that will stop the enemy in his tracks while retrieving it. It's your praise that will inevitably win this battle for you. Whenever something from your past rears up its ugly head, remind yourself of the goodness of God and praise your way through.

Please take note that praise is an action of the body, and worship is from the heart. During praise, one might raise one's hands, bow one's head, or do something physical. In worship, it is totally about our hearts being positioned in reverence to God's holy majesty. That means we don't have to feel good in order to praise. We simply have to do it, and worship will soon follow. Through every part of these battles, you must also remind yourself to not get weary in doing good and as a result turn from God's ways. Keep sowing good seed, and you'll soon start to see and reap a good harvest.

The last part of conquering this spiritual enemy is to not get discouraged when you don't see complete victory right away. In Exodus 23:29–30, God informs Israel that He will not drive out the Canaanites all at once but slowly, so that the land didn't become desolate and the animals didn't multiply against them. It was God's intention for Israel to be fruitful along this process and gain the land as they were ready. In the same way, God will not simply give the total annihilation of this enemy over to you. Your past, and the affects you carry from it, will not just go away; if they did, the promises God has for you will dry up or spoil because they'll become too numerous for you to handle. This is seen in the lesson learned in the wilderness by Israel when they would gather too much manna, and it would become rotten by the next day. Instead, these things will be brought to the surface purposefully in God's perfect timing, completely intended to be handled one at a time in order to keep you focused, growing, and fruitful. The One who knows all things will never give you more than you can take on. Whether things feel good or bad, His thoughts are higher, and His ways are better, which is why the first thing we do to achieve victory over this enemy is focus on Him.

Chapter 3

The Amorites

Overcoming the Past That Haunts You

The word of a testimony carries power. When Jehovah-Rapha heals someone, and that person chooses to share the story with others, it's in that moment that the grace for their healing can be received by someone else, and that person can then walk into that same healing power as well. The power of a testimony, when shared, transcends time and rushes into the present moment. However, in the same way a good report of something can bring uplifting and glorious results if received, the retelling of a bad event or situation can bring the exact opposite results—results like guilt, shame, and hurt. In some cases, people may even relive that moment and feel re-wounded, as if they were just going through it and freshly cut again. The rule of thumb is a testimony, based on the motive of the user, can be both used for either glory or destruction.

The stronghold where the Amorites live is a place called Gilead, which means "Heap of Testimony." The Amorites were descended from Canaan, so there's no coincidence that this battle bares its roots from the past as well. However, instead of being beat up by the past with guilt and shame like the spiritual tactics of the Canaanites, the Amorites represent the past being used against someone by someone. The power comes from not just others using your past against you but you yourself as well. The battle here is to make you believe you still are your past. The word of a testimony makes it as though the past is in the present and happening again right now. However, the key to that taking place is that the person has to receive it. A person can give an amazing deliverance testimony, and someone who needs that same deliverance can hear it, smile, not receive it, and walk away from that moment, never receiving the power of that testimony. In the same way, the devil, through the testimony of your past, has to convince you to receive the lies as though it is still you today. His trick is to block your mind from the truth of who you are and whose you are, so you will believe the lie that you still are who you were in the past. The constant truth for a believer is that you are no longer who you were; the blood of Jesus covers you, and you are a new creation. Even if Christians slip and stumble, they are no longer sinners who sinned but rather saints who sinned. The identity of a son and daughter of God is wrapped up in the One who died for them, and He has and continually will wash you clean. That truth is exactly what this enemy tries to draw you away from. This battle is a war between receiving or not receiving the bad things of the past that are being constantly held and used against you. The intention of the accuser is to keep you distraught and discouraged, to diminish vision, and to keep you in the same cycles. Moses faced the same Amorites that Joshua did but at a different time, which caused Israel to feel like they were caught in what probably seemed like a never-ending spiral.

The name Amorite means *talkers*, and this is where the spiritual influence of this enemy comes from: words! A person's words, when received, are very powerful. The Amorites were known to be as strong as oak trees and as tall as cedars. In the same way, the negative words spoken from your past seem to be the biggest and strongest testimonies known about you, and people often like to avoid these constant reminders with hopes to just move on. For Moses, he didn't want to fight this enemy either, and he tried to make peace with King Sihon, whose name is translated as *conclusion*. Often, we will try whatever it takes to not face something and come to the end of our struggle with the past. Just like Sihon did with Moses, we are refused that easy route, and we must stand strong. The Bible tells us that Israel defeated Sihon "with the edge of the sword." Immediately, your mind should remember Paul urging us to fight this spiritual war by taking up the sword of the Spirit, which is the Word of God. This is the path to victory and the only way to overcome the negative report of your past. It's not with praise like the Canaanites, but with the Word of God and the testimony that He declares over you. The memories themselves that haunt you from your past are very different from the spoken word about it in your present, and therefore the weapon used must be different too. If Israel tried to send Judah into battle against this enemy, God's people would have been defeated, but instead this mountain is won with scripture. Adam and Eve didn't have a clear understanding of who God said they were, and as a result they ate the fruit. In the same manner, as a Christian, if you don't know what the Creator says about you, then you too will eat the same fruit of lies the enemy spews at you. After all, who knows you better than the One who knows every fiber of your being and intricately knit you together in your mother's womb?

Moses sent spies to Jazer and went up to Bashan to face King Og after defeating King Sihon. Jazer means "Jehovah Helps," Bashan is translated as "in the tooth," and Og in its original Hebrew is "bread baked from ashes." It was there that God gave Israel the same command on how to defeat this set of Amorites. The answer was once again by the sword. This Amorite king lived in the tooth, which is located in a person's mouth and, like before, is centered around words. Your past doesn't simply go away because you overcome one part of it. This is another process, and in the same way you were instructed to declare the positive testimony of your Abba Father in order to be victorious in one Amorite battle, you must do this every time when someone recites negative memories against you. Eventually, there will be peace. But how can someone know for sure that they will eventually find peace? Because through Joshua, which is the English name for *Yeshua*, Elohim destroyed the fruit and the roots of the Amorites, and Israel finally walked into that peace. Israel attempted to bring themselves into peace under the leading of Moses, but it was Jehovah-Shalom who brought the peace they attempted to work for. It wasn't by their own working and fighting that they became victors, but when they listened and applied the instructions of the great I Am and used His word! That is the key to triumphing over the spiritual Amorites.

Chapter 4

The Hittites

Recognizing Fear

The devil is known for deception and distraction, and so were the Hittites. Deception goes far deeper than the spewing of simple lies. Tools like sophisticated manipulation, threatening, blackmail, and in-depth cons take deception to a level far greater than lying. At times, a lie can be felt and seen from miles away. Keeping that in mind, understanding comes as to the motivation of why the serpent was the craftiest out of all the animals. When someone takes the position of ignorance, arrogance, or desperation, that's when lies are formed, and the devil is none of these. Remember that he's not just a liar; his title goes way more in-depth than that, and he's known as the great deceiver. He is patient, and he doesn't mind letting the hills he planted in your life turn into Everests. Christians cannot allow themselves to be ignorant to how the enemy works. If he can make you think he's something he's not, then he's already won.

The Hittites had many names. Because they descended from Heth, they were also known as Hethites, and they were also called Nesites as well. Kittim was another name they used. They were an enemy who had many names and could play many different roles. The name *Heth* means *fear*, and the Hebrew name for *Hittites* is *terror.* These two names are the driving force, and the subconscious manipulation tactic of the enemy in this spiritual battle. Fear's plan of attack is to creep in using many different names: worry, anxiety, stress, dread, alarm, and being overly cautious. The Hittites represent fear, and for every Christian, fear is the root that cripples faith. It's that fear that cripples faith and always stops the move of God—until it's recognized and overcome.

This spiritual Hittite loves to disguise itself as a friend. Some Christians have been living with fear in their lives for so long that it seems to have grown to be a part of them. They're comfortable in it, and in some situations they don't even realize it's directing their decisions. They will use common excuses like "I'm just being careful" or "I'm taking my time because I just want to make the best choice." Another sneaky side effect of fear is overplanning, also known as procrastination and overthinking. There are even been believers who downplay fear by saying, "I'm not worrying; I'm just being cautious and guarding myself," not realizing that their hesitation is based around fear. These common sayings, and millions of variations like them, bring about the what-ifs that stir up doubt and, if not handled right away, lead to unbelief.

That tiny seed of fear is deposited in a person's heart by the smallest of situations. In every scenario, fear goes unrecognized because it is never the initial, outright attack of the enemy, but don't be fooled because it's always the result! Just like the Israelites were commanded to remove all traces of the Hittites, today's sons and daughters of God were instructed to not live in any hint of fear. If God's perfect love casts out all fear, then why does God tell His people to "fear not" more than any other command in the Bible? This could only be because the omniscient Creator of the universe knew what would be one of His children's greatest spiritual enemies.

The Hittites made their home in the hills around Hebron. *Hebron* in the original Hebrew language means *friendship.* Fear's greatest tactic is to make itself your friend, pretend it's helping you, and cause havoc from the inside out. Esau married Hittite women, Abraham bought his family burial ground from a Hittite, and the Hittites even lived among the Israelites for thousands of years. But probably the greatest Hittite known in the Bible was a warrior named Uriah. When most Christians think of Uriah, they often are met with pity and remorse because they think of Uriah as a loyal friend and faithful comrade who was betrayed. In reality, he and his people were enemies of Israel and we commanded by God to be removed back in the days of Joshua. Then why is he still there? David took one look at this Hittite's bathing wife, and the seed of fear was planted. Of course, it wasn't planted as fear itself, but it was that seed that led to the great hardships David faced after gazing upon Bathsheba. The enemy never hits us with fear head-on; he disguises it with attacks like lust, rape, adultery, mistrust, abuse, and all kinds of hurts, and in the end, it's those seeds that spring up and produce fear. David's adultery led to his constant worry and fear that people would know of his sin, and that led to death—maybe not for David directly, but for Uriah. For the Christian, our fear leads so often to spiritual death maybe not for us directly, but possibly for those closest to us like Uriah was to David. If we're called to walk in the Spirit with God, and fear counters faith and renders it inactive, then a believer's allowance of fear leads to faith without works, and faith without works is dead.

Fear is an alarming word, so of course the devil knows he can't simply plant it in a person and have it spring up roots. He has to deceive believers into thinking fear is on their side, or that what was just planted is not really fear at all by calling it something else less noticeable or threatening until it has enough time to grow. Then, just like Heth gave birth to the Hittites, when its fully grown, fear gives way to terror. Throughout the Bible, the Hittites were the hardest group to eliminate out of the life of Israel. They built cities among the Israelites, changed their names, turned into different people groups, and became a part of everyday life.

The Israelites never truly overcame the Hittites, and as a result, it caused them continuous problems even to this present day. Those with ears to hear can see the same path fear takes in a believer's mind if not dealt with. However, where Israel failed, we see how to bring about the victory. If a person steps right instead of left, and that right move is wrong, everyone then knows the best way to step is left. Through the recognition of Israel's errors, understanding and wisdom can be met head-on. So where exactly did the Israelites go wrong, and what was the instruction Yahweh gave that was intended to save them?

Time and time again, Israel failed to recognize the Hittites, and in the same manner, time and time again, Christians fail to recognize fear! Israel's failure to see the Hittites for who they really were led to them becoming a normal part of their lives and interacting with them like a small strand of virus. As Spirit-led children of God, we must recognize the seeds planted in our hearts that lead to or are from fear. Human beings don't become fearful all by themselves; there must be a cause that leads them to that fear first. Realizing what that seed is before it's planted is what Paul was talking about when he instructed the Corinthian church to cast down imaginations and every high thing that exalts itself against the knowledge of God. Paul knew that if God is love—and He absolutely is—then the knowledge and understanding of Him will remove all fear. Then Paul continued and told the church to bring into captivity every thought to the obedience of Christ. More simply put, believers must be guided and have a clear understanding of God's Word so that we can know the things that are right and wrong and recognize all the fiery darts of the enemy. That way they can be cast down before they even start to have roots. As mentioned before, the Word of God is a sword, but for a better mental image as to what kind of sword, picture a dagger. This dagger would be used on the battlefield in close combat. This is when the Christian has allowed the enemy to unknowingly get as close as only a friend should be. However, that wasn't the short sword's only use. It was also used to remove any arrows that broke through the armor and past their shield of faith. It makes a lot of sense to think that faith, the very thing used to stop fear, is the exact thing fear tries to kill. Whenever an arrow would fly past the shield and strike a warrior, they would take this dagger and dig it out. When the devil's fiery darts of deceptive fear fly past your shield of faith, you must use the Word of God to remind yourself of what the Father has established in, through, and around you. Dig out the wounds with the sharp words of scripture. Fear is crafty, deceiving, distracting, and disguising, and the sobering reality to that is sometimes people just don't see it coming. Therefore, it's important to know that the danger isn't being struck by it, but it's letting it become a part of you and learning to live with it. God's people were never intended to live in fear, although sometimes they may have to walk through its shadowy valley. But in those moments, Psalm 34 reminds us that when we seek the Lord, we can be sure He will answer, and He will deliver us from all our fears. God's Word can not only keep us from fear but also enable the people who use it to remove themselves from its deceptive clutches.

Chapter 5

The Hivites

The Enemy That Lives among You

When Elohim first explained to Moses His intention of giving His people the Promised Land that He promised to Abraham, Yahweh instructed Moses to completely dismantle the enemies who lived there. Then when Joshua stepped into leadership, God commanded him to do the same thing, which was to completely destroy the enemies that inhabited the land He was giving them. The Hivites were among those enemies, but they were not as foolish as the rest. The Hivites were known as the craftiest of the enemies Israel had to face. They lived by Mount Hermon, which means "devoted to destruction," in the land of Shechem, which one of the most common translations for this word is *consent*. This is ironic but not coincidental, considering that in their cunning, scheming ways, they eluded their fate of total destruction by gaining consent from Israel to stay in the land. The Hivites heard of the great victories that Israel had won over the other enemies, and they devised a plan. They didn't oppose Israel in battle at first; rather, they decided to trick them into believing they were peaceful travelers coming to worship the Lord. In other words, these sneaky foes came in the name of the Lord! The Hivites knew that no one can come against God and His command for Israel to destroy all the people in the land. In order to not be eradicated, they conjured up a plan to make peace, and by the time Israel realized who they were, the sons and daughters of God had already sworn an oath and given them consent to live among them.

The Hivites represent a battle that hits the believer from both angles and is both a spiritual and physical attack. The Hivites dressed themselves in different clothes and pretended to come from a far-off land. This enemy will depict itself as something familiar, often painting the picture of a victim or someone in need of God's wisdom. The Hivite targets the Christian's hunger to help and guide, and even their eagerness to be used by God. This is the very door it uses to gain access into one's life. Physically, these are the people who slowly slide themselves into the congregation and into a believer's life, by means of friendship or victim mentality, needing what the excited-to-help Christian has. From the inside, they lead Christians astray. The Hivites approached Israel with worn clothes and dried bread to prove they were in need and desperate for a touch from God. They came with words of peace but with a real motivation of self-survival and eventually war. The Hivite spirit's goal is to shake things up and to cause strife, separation, murmuring, doubt, and debates among friends, churches, marriages, and even family members. In this battle, the key tactic for the enemy is to feed into whatever Christians want to hear, whether it's them helping, guiding, receiving praise or attention, their desire to be taught, or even their need for companionship. Spiritually, it will wage war against believers' minds, causing self-doubt, stagnated growth, and eventually faithlessness. This is the most conniving way for the devil to steal, kill, and destroy a Christian's goals and purpose. It's a slow work that often, as in the case of Joshua, goes unnoticed until it's living as a neighbor in your midst.

The enemy knows his time is near and that he is in a battle he cannot win, so his plan of attack is to slip his way into a Christian's everyday life under the illusion that he is a peacemaking friend.

The Bible says that the devil portrays himself as an angel of light: something good, holy, and welcoming. The hardest enemy to recognize is the enemy who switches sides. The devil has a really good understanding of how everything works; after all, he's been here since the beginning, and he started off on the side of truth. This is why believers must sharpen the gift of discernment and learn to trust it. The Holy Spirit is always speaking, warning, guiding, and convicting everyone of sin and righteousness. It's the churches' responsibility to polish that spiritual gift so there is no room for the enemy to slip in unexpectedly. This is the path to victory over this Hivite opponent. As followers of Christ, we are supposed to reflect the image of Jesus to the rest of the world. It is Holy Spirit's job to lead us into that glorious transformation day by day. This is what it means to work out your salvation with honor and the understanding that it is not the Christian's ability to complete the requirements of God, but a surrendering to the Holy Spirit so He can bring about the already finished work. Jesus Christ is God, but He put off His divinity and walked out His ministry as a man, clothed and empowered by the Holy Spirit. Everything He did, He did by the guidance of Holy Spirit. When the Bible recalls the times that the Pharisees would try to slip their way into His life and cause debate and doubt, it's recorded that Jesus would perceive what their intentions were and not fall into their traps. When one of His closest friends, Peter, told Him that death would not be His fate, He was able to recognize, through discernment, the attempt of the devil to steer Him away from His purpose, and He rebuked the spirit but not the person. Our Savior repeatedly relied on the prompting of the Holy Spirit to overcome His Hivite battles, so how much more do Christians as well?

The most important tool for victory over this enemy is to understand that Jesus wasn't simply given the Holy Spirit at the Jordan River and that's all it took. Jesus honored, nurtured, and continuously built that relationship! He would separate Himself, wake up early, go to sleep late, and constantly be obedient to whatever Holy Spirit told Him to do. These aren't the only keys to building a solid bond with the Spirit of God, but it's the Bible's way of telling every believer that Jesus did whatever it took to reverence the precious gift of the Holy Spirit. Yes, God's Spirit will never leave you or forsake you, but that doesn't mean that Christians can turn a deaf ear to Him and numb His promptings. Honoring and building a relationship with the Holy Spirit and allowing Him to become the leader of your life is the key to this entire Christian walk, and it's the answer to beating your physical and spiritual Hivites. It's the Holy Spirit that will give you the gift of discernment and then teach you how to grow in it and use it. It's Holy Spirit that will give you the ability to recognize the Hivites before they become your neighbor. And it's the precious Holy Spirit that will help you remove them if they've already infiltrated your life. For the Israelites, God sent swarms of hornets to drive out the Hivites, and all that God's people had to do was remain faithful and in communion with the angel that was sent before them to lead and guide them. For the Christian today, that "angel" was a type of foreshadowing of the Holy Spirit! His discernment and His leading is the answer against which the Hivites don't stand a chance.

Chapter 6

The Philistines

Stolen Praise

The Philistines were the most relentless enemy that Israel faced. They are referenced throughout the entire Old Testament and still had remaining traces of descendants in the New Testament. They were a constant annoyance to God's people, and every time they were thought to be defeated, that persistent enemy would raise its ugly head again years later. The name Philistine means *invader*, yet their tactic was always intimidation. They were a very big, strong people, they were smart, well established, and advanced in technology. This made them an extremely difficult foes to overcome both mentally and physically.

The greatest battle recorded in the Bible, and the one that gives the most information on this spiritual opponent, is the face-off between David and the towering Philistine Goliath. It's here, in the details of this battle, that the motivation and the tactics of the devil are discovered. The Philistine army waged war against Israel in a location that did not belong to them. It was the land allotted to the tribe of Judah, and as already previously mentioned, *Judah* means *praise*. This is the goal of this enemy: to steal your praise. As Christians, we enter God's presence with praise and thanksgiving; it's what positions the heart for worship. Fellowship and relationship with God is the main reason for the sacrifice of Christ, so praise is a very essential tool in the Christian walk. If the enemy can take away your motivation to praise God, he not only opens the door for that Canaanite spirit we first talked about to bring an onslaught of past mistakes rushing back to memory, but he also shifts the focus off of God, attempts to sever relationship, and fixes your eyes onto the giants that stand before you so you feel helpless and alone. The tactic is to first intimidate you and then invade your thoughts. Everything about Goliath was daunting and terrifying, from his nine foot nine stature to the shining bronze armor that weighed over 5,600 shekels (1,200 pounds). That was why the Israelite army ran and cowered in fear.

Goliath would mock and discourage the children of God, and that's exactly what this enemy does to Christians. The goal is to depress, dishearten, and break the hopes of the believers, leaving them so downtrodden and energy deficient that they lose focus and relinquish the will to praise. This allows the past to sneak in, the problems of today to overwhelm you, and the thoughts of tomorrow to seem extremely tiring. This is spiritual suffocation at its greatest level. The very thought of the enemy the believer sees standing before them is big, scary, and unbeatable, and this takes the once on fire, Holy Spirit–breathing Christians into a place where they start to question their identity in Christ and even the salvation they received from Him. The result can easily be what we see in Israel throughout the entire Old Testament: them bending to the will of the Philistines.

It's obvious to see through the story of Israel that this enemy is not simply defeated once and then never seen and heard from again; it's an enemy that will try to invade the minds of believers throughout their entire lives. So how is this enemy overcome and sent running as the sons and daughters of God plunder its camp? Once again, the answer is found in the courageous story of David verses Goliath. David knew who he was, and knew the enemy he faced. The Philistines had five cities, and Goliath was the champion of Gath, one of those cities. In addition, Goliath also had four sons. David knew this wasn't the only time he would face a Philistine enemy, which was why he picked up five rocks from the brook: one rock for each city, or a rock for Goliath and then one for each of his sons. Upon hearing the blasphemous shouts of Goliath, David decided to take a stand in the name of the Lord. When opposed by Saul and reminded of his weaknesses and disadvantages, David simply brought back to his remembrance all the victories he already had won in his life. It's important to know that this Philistine spirit will not only try to intimidate your mind, but it will also try to intimidate and influence the minds of those around you in order to shift your perspective of how big the obstacle is you face and of the things that disqualify you from overcoming it. For the shepherd boy, he simply thought back to the lion and the bear he'd slain while tending sheep for his father. Like David, every believer must remember and focus on the previous victories they've had while the enemy tries to distract them with the fight that stands before them. David encouraged himself by focusing on the fact that in the same way God delivered him from the lion and the bear, God could and would deliver this giant into his hands. This was why he wrote that even though he walked through the Valley of Elah, he would fear no evil, and he reminded himself that his head was anointed with oil and his destiny wasn't to fall at the hand of this uncircumcised Philistine; it was to be seated as king over Israel.

Once again, just like for David, it's not by sword and spear that this battle will be won today. The key to this victory is to remind yourself not only of the previous victories you've overcome in your past but also of the promises God has laid before you. Once Goliath fell, David ran to him, drew out that Philistine's own sword from its sheath, and cut the giant's head off. One of the very weapons Goliath planned to use against Israel was used to claim the victory. When that spiritual Philistine attack tries to steal your praise by reminding you of your past, attempting to shift your focus on the current problems of today and exhaust the plans of your future, simply use those weapons against the enemy and remind yourself of the previous victories you've won. Change your perspective of how you see the enemy. Focus on where God has promised to take you! This battle is not yours—it's the Lords. Although you may sit at a table, feeling surrounded by enemies, always remember, your cup is running over, and surely mercy and goodness will follow you all the days of your life. Remind yourself of the victories you've already claimed, and don't stop praising!

Chapter 7

The Midianites, the Moabites, and the Ammonites

Inner-circle Betrayal

Abraham is known as the father of many nations because of his unwavering faith and trust in God. When Yahweh brought Abraham face-to-face with a choice that would make most men turn and run away from the promises God has for them, he was willing to sacrifice his only beloved son, Isaac. It was in that moment that Abraham truly walked into covenant and promise with the Creator of the universe. What an honor that was! However, as history tells us, it was Abraham's son Isaac who was given the blessing to carry on the family name and the privilege to represent and reflect God's entrusted covenant in the earth. Every believer knows the story of Isaac and his brother Ishmael, and if you ask one of those believers whom Abraham was married to, their answer would undoubtedly be Sarah. However, the family line didn't end with Sarah, Isaac, and Ishmael. When Sarah died, Abraham was married again to a woman named Keturah, and they had six sons together. One of those sons was named Midian! The Midianites were descendants of Midian and therefore children of Abraham. In other words, the Midianites were family.

Like for Israel, this spiritual attack of the enemy comes from the ones closest to us: family or those close friends who feel like family—the very ones who were allowed into our inner circle. This spiritual attack is betrayal at its deepest, and this spirit influences those closest to you to cast the knife far into your back. These attacks of treachery may not be the biggest wounds, but they are the deepest, and they most definitely hurt the most!

The name *Midianite* means *strife*, and this is the exact goal of the Midianite spirit: to bring strife, discord, disagreement, and separation. The main thing to understand with this enemy is that the betrayal may come from someone close, but it's through the influence of a very strong spirit. Therefore do not focus on the person; instead, focus on the fact that this is a spiritual battle. The Midianites were always very close with the Israelites. When Moses killed the Egyptian and fled from the wrath of Pharaoh, he ran away to Midian. It was there that he met and married his wife, Zipporah, and served his father-in-law, Jethro, for forty years as a shepherd. As we read in Exodus 2, Jethro was a Midianite priest, which tells us that the Midianites still held onto some kind of knowledge of the God from their father, Abraham. It was this connection that, when the Israelites were traveling in the desert, led to Moses being able to employ the services of his brother-in-law, Hobab. Hobab was familiar with the land and was therefore able to serve as a guide.

In the context of a spiritual view, the Midianite spirit will target those who have been there through the toughest of times— the ones who are the closest to you and have even given you the greatest amount of direction while you are walking out the process God has given you. They are cut from the same cloth and can even be from within your very church. So yes, this means that even your pastor and other spiritual leaders can unknowingly be influenced by this spirit, and even you yourself can fall victim to this sneaky spirit as well. The goal of this enemy is to bring such friction between you and those close to you that a once strong bond is now severed, and arguments and offense can easily break out. For Israel, their relationship with the Midianites took a turn for the worse when this once close friend sided with the Moabites in order to hire Balaam and curse them.

We also see this same spirit at work in the New Testament. Judas was one of Jesus's inner circle and closest friends. At one time, Jesus referred to His disciples as His brothers. Because Judas did not agree and understand Jesus's approach to victory, he sided with the high priests and betrayed his once closest friend. For believers, just like with Judas, we see that as soon as its work of influence is done and the strife and separation is caused, this spirit leaves the victims to stew in the remnants of their battle. Both the influenced and the victim are left wondering why the argument was taken so far, and they're both left feeling like there's nothing that can be done to restore this now broken relationship.

That said, this is a perfect place to completely expose the targets of this evil spirit. This attack is not only a betrayal against people but a direct onslaught against love as well. Let's be quickly reminded that love is patient and kind; it doesn't envy or boast, and it's not proud. It doesn't dishonor others or seek out its own victory. It's not easily angered, and it doesn't keep any record of the wrongs done against it. Love doesn't delight in evil, but it rejoices when the truth prevails. Love always trusts, hopes, and preserves, and it never gives up! This Midianite spirit is an all-out attack in every way on love Himself. God has built us to love one another, and this enemy blinds your eyes to patience and kindness while making both sides believe they are right. It fuels the flame of anger by dishonoring one another and planting the need to win the fight! This is exactly what leads to grudges and reciting past hurts. This spirit breaks down trust, hope, and the will to keep the relationship together. This spirit results in the exact opposite of love!

So what do you do when you see the results of this spirit infiltrating your inner circle, or when you realize it already has? God gave a set of specific instructions to Israel, and when they carried them out, they walked into effortless victory. Jesus also demonstrated these instructions perfectly after His betrayal.

God told Israel to gather one thousand men from every tribe and attack the Midianites. The number one thousand always biblically represents divine completeness. Yahweh's instruction to gather the one thousand men is another way of saying that God instructed every tribe to unite completely. Not only were the people of Israel in one accord, but the priests brought articles from the sanctuary and a trumpet for signaling. The obedience of Israel to these instructions was the greatest way they stepped into victory against the Midianites!

What this means spiritually for believers today is that community is your best and most effective weapon against this enemy. It's not just community by itself, doing nothing, but a community that will wage war in prayer together, in one accord. Sure, prayer at home, in your secret place, or in the shower will bring great breakthrough and revelation in many areas, but this specific enemy needs to be fought hand in hand with others, with everyone agreeing together in one mind and one heart. When Jesus was betrayed by Judas, where did He go? Straight to His favorite place of prayer, the garden of Gethsemane. If you remember, for Christians, the garden is not a place but represents the spirit, and we see that Jesus immediately goes to the garden to pray. However, notice that He did not go alone; He told his disciples to pray as well. Jesus loved to pray alone! He woke up early and went to bed late just to get some alone time with the Father. But this was not an alone-time prayer, and to come against this enemy, Jesus needed community, so He told His disciples to pray as well. In the same way, if our Lord and Savior, the One who walked everything out perfectly, needed community against this enemy and the sting of betrayal, how much more do believers today need community?

The Fight Continues

For Israel, this wasn't the end of their battle with the Midianites. The children of God, upon victory, decided to keep the women and children, which was directly against the instructions of God to completely destroy them. It's important to know that the word *destroy* represents not killing off every person but destroying the name or image of the people, in turn rendering the enemy powerless. When Christians face an adversary, there's often a temptation to keep things alive and brewing and in the background of their thinking. It's this "I'll forgive, but I won't forget" mentality that gives a foothold for this Midianite spirit to again raise its ugly head in the future. However, as stated in previous chapters, Israel's errors lead to today's insights and victories. The Midianites terrorized Israel for hundreds of years as a result of them keeping people and things alive—that is, until God sent a judge named Gideon. Many know the brave story of Gideon and how God narrowed his army down from thirty-two thousand to just three hundred men. This shows believers the last, but very critical, aspect to defeating this Midianite enemy: to be selective about whom you choose to be in your community of prayer partners. The last thing you want is to have your community sleeping while you're praying for your life!

This enemy is tough, and it loves to squeeze its way into your mind and into the minds of those around you. It loves to influence and cause strife that leads to separation and painful division. Even after its defeat, if allowed, it loves to linger, waiting for an opportunity to pick at old wounds. Although it places a root inside those it hurts to not trust people and whispers the lie that it's better to not let people close, this is exactly what is needed: a close community that will stay alert, focused, and determined in prayer to see victory as your outcome. This enemy is conquered by a close community focused in prayer!

The Moabites

There is a reason why there are three enemies combined in this chapter. These enemies came together as one against Israel, and in the same way, these three spirits invite each other into the onslaught against Christians spiritually. This means one open door leads to another open door, and one spiritual attack opens the door to a stronger, more specific spiritual attack. All three of these nations worshiped the same deity, and they fed off of the victories of the others. Simply saying, if Israel was attacked by one, they were attacked by the others as well, and when Israel allowed one of these nations into its circle, they unknowingly allowed the other two. For the believer today, spiritually this means when you're attacked by one of these spirits, there's a chance that you'll be attacked by the other two as well, unless the attack is stopped. If you allow one spirit influence for your mind, you unknowingly allow the other two.

These attacks are still rooted in betrayal from your inner circle, which is the Midianite spirit. The attack of the Midianite spirit opens the door for an attack from the Moabite spirit, which is a deeper, more specific, and direct attack of betrayal. This Moabite spirit still targets the inner circle, but now the betrayal comes in the form of molestation, incest, or rape; it could also be from the rejection of the father or the mother. This is no longer just a general disloyalty and a stabbing in the back; this is a specific attack in these areas. The name *Moabite* means "of his father" and *destroyer*. This attack most commonly comes from a parent, a close and trusted family member, or a parental figure; it's mainly implemented while Christians are still children (under the age of twelve); and it's always a form of sexual assault, which is intended to destroy and rip apart families. Again, it is very important to realize that this is a spiritually influenced attack! That's why the breach of trust comes from those who are closest. These people start out full of love and good intentions, but then they become influenced (as believers) or even possessed (as non-believers) by these spirits. This is where the now demonically influenced thoughts become manifested, and the betrayal takes place. Take note that where you allow one of these spirits, the other two will be invited as well. They all carry the same motives and tactics, and therefore they want to remain hidden. The most common way people will allow this spirit to unknowingly remain attached to them is by being deceived into keeping these certain betrayals a secret. In the case of many sexual attacks, either the victim is convinced to stay quiet, or the shame that attaches itself to the attack causes the person to not tell anyone; the belief that no one will believe them causes them to try to fight the painful results of this betrayal on their own. Keep in mind that the only way to overcome this spirit is with prayer within trusted community. Demons are sneaky, and if they can convince the assaulted party that they are alone, then there won't be any kind of community sought out, and that demonic attack will linger and have open-door access to the thoughts and memories of that injured and betrayed person. This Moabite spirit is still betrayal, but it is a very specific type of betrayal centered around sexual assault coming from someone in the inner circle. The answer to breaking off this spirit, forever closing the door to its reluctant influence, and walking into freedom and victory is to expose it within a trusted community that will cover you in prayer and support. Keep in mind that the cover-up and the secrecy surrounding this attack give legal right for that spirit to stay, and that's exactly what it wants to do!

The Ammonites

Both the Moabites and the Ammonites came from an incestuous union between Lot and his daughters. This spirit is the most depraved and twisted spirit of the three, and it roots itself in the sneakiest and most subtle forms of betrayal! The main deity worshipped by the Ammonites was Molech; the Moabites called it Chemosh. This idol had the head of a calf and outstretched human arms for accepting baby sacrifices. This bronze statue would be heated with fire, into which the victims were thrown.

The Ammonites were just as cruel and corrupt as the false god they worshipped, and they were known for gouging out eyes and ripping open pregnant women. This is exactly the target of this spiritual attack. The main goal of this spirit is to remove the vision and the purpose of God's people. The main tactic to eliminate purpose is that prior to birth, it causes miscarriages and influences abortions. After birth, there's the destruction and breakdown of children's minds to separate them and leave them feeling rejected, abandoned, and alone. If this spirit can't influence abortion, then it will influence the parents to reject and abandon their children. This spirit is the exact reason why there is such a rise in Plan B pills, abortions, and absentee parents in the world today.

As previously mentioned, this spirit is the most sly and crafty of the three! It roots itself in lies and deep deception, and it is the direct result of the sexual assault the influencing Moabite spirit brings. In rape and molestation victims who become pregnant, this spirit convinces the women to abort the child, thus eliminating the purpose God Himself has given that baby. Yes, the pregnancy may have come from an unfortunate and demonically influenced event, but God is still the Creator of life, and He has given purpose to every human being, born and unborn. If a child is conceived, no matter how it's conceived, it has a purpose given to him or her by the Author of the universe, and any attempt to eliminate that living baby is an attempt to eliminate its God-given purpose. Yes, the circumstances that brought about the pregnancy are terrible, but the baby should not be the one who's punished. The inerrant stance of pro-choice laws delicately and precisely go against the knowledge that God orchestrates life and that if there is life, there is purpose, and Yahweh has a plan in the midst of it all. This is a subtle and often unrecognized tactic of the enemy to bring about a false-positive reasoning for abortion. It convinces people that the specific circumstances surrounding the pregnancy can determine the choice that can be made regarding life and death. This audacious stance actually places people in the position of

God, which is blasphemy and idolatry wrapped up in one act. This clever and cunning spirit has now influenced and gained enough access to eliminate purpose, and it caused someone to stand in rebellion against the plans and design of the great I Am, which later can cause guilt and condemnation.

This spirit also settles its roots in the lineage of a family and is the cause of a generational curse that causes miscarriages. When this common occurrence of miscarriages is recognized in a family, the door must be closed by prayer, declaration, and pleading the blood of Jesus Christ over the known or unknown events that opened the door in the first place. The target of this prayer must be the first act of betrayal in the family line. If you don't know the first place this slimy serpent slid in, then you can simply declare that wherever the door was opened that it be shut and that the line of influence and access be cut off. If the enemy can stop life from coming forth through abortion or miscarriages, his ultimate goal and attack against God and humanity is already completely. If life comes into the world, it can always be influenced by good, which in turn breaks the grip of influence the demonic has over it. Light always overpowers darkness! Each person is given vision and purpose, and as long as there is life and breath, that purpose can still come to pass. If the devil can stop or end life through influence, generational curses, or any avenue, he doesn't have to worry about those people following the God-given plans for which they were created.

These three spirits combine together to form the greatest hostile assault against all of humanity. They root themselves in betrayal and focus on the breakdown and the decimation of vision and purpose. The only rightful and effective retaliation against them is submerging yourself in community prayer. Prayer rightfully positions us by giving us the mind and heart of our Abba Father. Community prayer takes it further, narrows the sights to target a specific topic and situation, and brings together people in unity and strength against a common enemy or attack.

There are some situations where one-on-one prayer time with your heavenly Father will work just fine, but there are these three spirits that can only be broken by being united in one accord with selected people whom you trust.

Prayer over Those Who Have Had Abortions

While writing this chapter, the Holy Spirit weighed in heavy on my heart for those who may be reading this book and have had an abortion. There is no guilt and condemnation in Jesus Christ! When He was put to death, Romans 4:25 tells us that Jesus was delivered and died for our transgressions. That word *transgressions* in its original context means unintentional errors and willful transgressions. That simply means the things you know you're doing wrong, as well as the things you don't know you're doing wrong and you do out of ignorance. Whatever the reasoning behind your decision, whether it be selfish, fear, or ignorance, or if you were convinced that it was the right thing to do, it doesn't matter! Jesus paid for it, and you can boldly and proudly stand before the Father, totally clean of that decision with no more guilt and shame. There is no judgment that your heavenly Father holds against you, because Jesus Christ bore that judgment for you! God loves to restore things, so I encourage you to put this broken thing in His hands and see what the Creator of all things can make out of it.

Father, I pray for the ones reading this book whose hearts are sad and weighed down with the guilt and condemnation of their decision to influence abortion, or to have an abortion. I pray Your peace over them right now in the name of Jesus Christ. I declare that Your love surrounds them and that the weight of this circumstance be lifted off their shoulders. Holy Spirit, remind them that each and every day, they are made new, and if the Father doesn't hold an account of their transgressions, neither should they! Remind them and let them feel the tangible touch of Your forgiveness. Lead them into forgiveness for themselves. I cancel guilt, condemnation, and self-hatred, and I replace it with Your unconditional love. I rebuke the Midianite, Moabite and Ammonite spirits, and I command them to release their hold on God's people, in the name of Jesus Christ! Holy Spirit, fill up those who feel empty because of the influence these spirits had over them. I break the power of these spirits, and I command the hearts and minds of all those reading this to submit to the Lordship of Holy Spirit. I declare victory and freedom in the name and for the glory of Yeshua the Christ! Amen.

Chapter 8

The Edomites

The Most Common Spiritual Enemy

Let's start out by saying this is the most complex chapter in this book. In order to understand this enemy and how it operates and infiltrates, there must be an in-depth understanding of who and what this spirit actually is. That said, the Edomites will be broken down thoroughly because this is the most common spirit overlooked by all humankind, especially the Church. Consequently, this spirit does the most damage and is the root of every wrong decision a Christian will make! The Edomites represent the spirit of compromise.

The Edomites descended from Esau, the brother of Jacob, who sold his birthright for a piece of bread and a pot of lentil stew. Esau compromised what was his rightful inheritance for a "right here, right now" satisfaction. As Christians, this is what happens every time we enter into sin! The Bible says that sin is only pleasurable for a moment or a season, and that there's a way that seems right to a man but in the end leads to death. When faced with immediate gratification, people have a tendency to choose what's in front of their face at the moment instead of what they know is right or the promises given to them by God. Sometimes the timing of the promise is not the timing of the individual, or maybe it's doubting that the promise will ever come to pass. Whatever the reason, often the very promise that's being waited on is traded away for something far less. In this case, you have unknowingly accepted the counterfeit because it's conveniently there now. Whenever you accept the counterfeit of anything, you will *never* see the real thing! This is the goal of the spirit of compromise. It's the same spirit that Adam and Eve fell victim to in the garden when they chose to compromise what they already had for what they felt they were missing out on. The root of compromise in believers' minds actually declares and proves their lack of trust in the Almighty God in that specific area. For example, if people rob a bank, it's because they don't believe God will provide, and they need it right here and right now. When we enter into sinful actions, we're compromising the promises God Himself has spoken over us, thus taking life into our own hands and saying that we know better than the omnipotent, all-knowing God, Yahweh.

The Edomite spirit bares much deeper roots than what it would have you believe. The name *Edom* means *red*. Red has a very specific meaning throughout the Bible. Whenever something is repeated, or when a color or number is mentioned, it's God's way of using nonverbal communication and inviting us to venture a little deeper into His understanding. As for the color red, it symbolizes atonement, sacrifice, life, death, and flesh. In the original Hebrew, it's also used in connection to the words *adom*, which means humankind or to make; *chakliy*, which means dark or a person influenced by wine; and *suph*, which is translated as a reed (in reference to the Red Sea). The word *red* is always used when either man himself fell into compromise or when God had to redeem the shortcomings and compromises of man. The most important use of symbolism with the color red is used to indicate the atoning blood of Jesus Christ! This was Elohim's ultimate cover-up for sin, which sin is derived from a choice of compromise.

This spiritual enemy's goal is to influence any size compromise in order to steer believers and nonbelievers alike away from destiny and purpose. Whether it be a subtle, small compromise or an enormous, blatant lack of holy reverence, compromise is compromise, and this sneaky spirit will take whatever it can get. The first place Edom comes against Israel is in the book of Numbers. It's there when the Israelites request passage through Edomite territory, and the king of Edom refuses safe travel and threatens Israel with war. Israel tries to barter with Edom, but the king refused to give into any of the Israelite's requests. This is a huge revelation to understand when battling this spirit! Christians cannot make deals with compromise because this spirit is simply looking for a reason to cause a bigger problem. Ironically, this Edomite spirit of compromise will never compromise itself. It's also important to know that this is a clever and conniving spirit that never has intentions of going away. It is not a spirit that you can gain deliverance from, or overcome once and never face again. This is a spirit that will continually look for influence over your every decision. Whether it be in a complex, or even common every day choice, it must be recognized and dealt with each time it rears its hideous head. The tactic of compromise is to try to influence every decision a person will make so that the true will of God is never reached fully.

The Edomites also teamed up with Babylon, which shows us the most common string compromise will pull on when trying to influence someone's choices. Babylon always represents pride and confusion in the Bible. Babylon is rooted in pride, and its results always lead to confusion. The first place Babylon is mention is with the Tower of Babel. A closer look into the original Hebrew translation of Genesis 11:4 will explain how the Tower of Babel was not just a tower but really much more. Verse four reads as follows.

> And they commanded, "Come, let us construct,
> build and establish for ourselves a city and town,
> and a strong place, a bed of flowers, a pulpit,

> a tower with its top to the heavens. And make
> for ourselves a name and reputation, lest we be
> scattered and dispersed abroad on the face of all
> the Earth."

The construction of this city and town consisted of much more than just a tower; it held all the facets of who God wants to be in a person's life.

A strong place represents a city of refuge. A city of refuge was a location where perpetrators of accidental manslaughter could claim the right of asylum. If a person killed another person, that person was deserving of death. As Christians, the Bible tells us that the wages of sin are death. Yahweh sent His Son so that He can be our city of refuge, the strong place that we run to for salvation! A bed of flowers is symbolism for a garden, which represents God's presence, provision, and purpose. A pulpit is anything used to release the words and teachings of God; whether it be a platform, a street corner, a social media page, or a book, if it's used to spread the gospel of Jesus Christ, it's a pulpit. Anytime preachers use a pulpit for their own gain and not the glorification of Jesus Christ and the revelation of the Father's heart, they run the risk of God scattering that pulpit just like He did with Babel. The pulpit is used for God's work, never our own! And lastly, Proverbs 18:10 tells us that the name of the Lord is a strong tower, and the righteous man runs into it and is safe. This closer look at what Babel really was reveals why God was forced to scatter such a prideful and idolatrous city! Everything that was built in Babylon was full of idolatry and self-centeredness and surrounded with pride! Compromise will always attach itself to anything that tries to take the place of God, and it will make people feel as if they know more than the One who created them in the first place.

The greatest fall of Israel was predicted by the prophet Isaiah when King Hezekiah showed off the riches of Judah to Babylon. Pride comes before the fall, just like what happened continuously with Israel and its leaders. So, don't be fooled. Be aware that the spirits of pride, complacency, idolatry, and selfishness are always connected to the Edomite spirit of compromise!

What to Do

Now that this spirit is exposed, let's take a look at how Israel was able to physically overcome it so there can be spiritual freedom from the Edomites for God's children today as well. Israel constantly ignored Edom. They went out of their way to go around the land of the Edomites, and they even turned back and didn't proceed forward when standing at their border. This worked only temporarily and only caused bigger issues in Israel's future. This is a huge caution to all Christians! There can be no retreat or ignoring this spirit. The Edomites eventually teamed up with Israel's other enemies and overtook the children of God later on down the road. Notice how compromise, no matter how big or small, will always lead you into other struggles and hardships when you choose to walk in it. If you pretend that you're not compromising, or if you are trying to ignore the places you are compromising, you will eventually fall victim to the venomous bite of this cobra. The only answer to victory over this spirit is found in the triumph David achieved in 2 Samuel 8:14. David built garrisons throughout Edom, and all the Edomites became David's servants.

Spiritually, this battle is in the mind of the believer, so there must be garrisons built in the mind. A garrison is a fortress equipped with troops in order to defend it. The sons and daughters of the King no longer fight with physical swords, but every Christian's sword is the Word of God! Paul tells us in Romans that as brothers and sisters of Jesus Christ, we must have renewed and transformed minds. The more people read God's Word, reflecting on His promises and standards, the more garrisons that will be built throughout their minds that will counter the temptation and influence of compromise. For every fortress that's built, that's one less area of influence the spirit of compromise can convince you to relinquish your command. This spirit is unrelenting and never backs down. It looks for any place to slip its way in.

As Christians, there must be no place or foothold given to the enemy that can be influenced by the Edomite spirit; that's why it's imperative to renew your mind daily and consistently be in the Word of God! Memorize, meditate, and put into action everything you read in the Bible. Bring it before God and allow the Holy Spirit to lead you further than you ever imagined going. Allow every line of scripture to become personal and written specifically for you. Every word and every verse are your valuable possessions, so cherish them all dearly in your heart. This is the key to victory over the Edomites!

Chapter 9

The Amalekites

A Warning for Church Leadership

This spirit is the main cause of dysfunction, division, and lack of individual church growth. It has been there since the church was planted but doesn't rise to power until things are established and underway. The Amalekite spirit has no problem being recognized and called out simply because it feeds off of controversy and accusation. The Amalekites came from Amalek, who descended from Eliphaz, Esau's son. They were not established at the same time as the other enemies of Israel; they arose to power long after all the other nations. Ironically, even though it was the last enemy to be established, it was the first enemy to attack Israel. As soon as Israel left Mount Sinai and started their journey toward the Promised Land, the Amalekites attacked those who were grumbling and weary and falling behind. This is the same tactic this spirit uses in the church today. It waits for the church to be established and underway, and then it attacks by influencing the members and causing them to complain against the leadership. This in turn causes the heads of the church to become very exhausted and overwhelmed, often leading to compromise, giving up, or a lack of motivation.

Deuteronomy 25:19 reminds us that when Israel was weary

and worn out, it was at that time when they were met by this adversary. This gives us a tremendous glimpse into what this spirit's favorite target is, and when you know your enemy, you can better defend against it! The type of leadership this spirit brings an attack against is leadership that has taken on too much and is tired, overwhelmed, and overworked, which makes room for the spirit to influence complaining. This could be a result of the leaders not delegating responsibility properly or not assigning the correct people in the proper areas, thus still requiring the leaders to take on the heavy load of all the work. With that said, let one of the biggest lies of the devil be addressed so there is no leadership that is tricked into believing that there isn't anyone in the church who can help. If God has granted you the ability to start a church, He has also brought the help you need to run and sustain it. You simply have to open your eyes to see what and who He has already placed within your reach. He not only used the staff Moses was already carrying, but He opened his eyes up to see the gift of speech his brother Aaron possessed; He gave Elijah his predecessor, Elisha; He brought Ruth to an old and widowed Naomi; and when David was being hunted by Saul, Elohim put a zeal and passion in the heart of Jonathan that would save his life continuously. God has already given you everything you need to succeed. All you have to do is recognize it!

Do not open any doors for this spirit to enter your church and remain there. It doesn't matter how exhaustion makes its way into the life of the leadership; the simplest way to defuse and shorten the influence of this spirit is by the church's leadership not taking on too much work, which means delegation and relying on others, and by not talking against your church leadership for any reason, whether you feel they're right or wrong. The main goal of the Amalekite spirit is to grumble and complain about how things are being performed inside the four walls of the church. This forms division among members, creates cliques within the church, and removes the attention off of what the real focus of the church should be, which is to be the alive and active demonstration of the Father's love to a lost and broken world. This deceitful spirit makes people focus on what's wrong with the church instead of what's wrong with the hurting people around it and inside it. There is no perfect church, so here will always be something wrong. It makes small problems look and feel huge, resulting in the important problems seeming miniscule and in need of less attention.

The Amalekite spirit is very contagious! It can and will influence as many people as it can. It's the very virus inside many churches that lead to their doors closing. A virus left untreated will overrun and eventually destroy everything to which it's connected. Whoever shows this evil spirit attention and is involved in the moaning and protesting, which includes the leadership itself, can fall victim to its devastating consequences. A virus's objective it to breakdown and destroy its host, which is why public rebuke only fuels this spirit's fire. This is the simplest way for this spirit to cause more division and ridicule. It's a master at twisting the truth and redistributing blame. Therefore, it is very important that once it's recognized, it must be handled in private!

Now, whenever Israel faced this enemy, they always kept the defeated king alive, they took plunder for themselves, and then they lied about their reasons for doing so. This error is a great warning for the church today. When this spirit is exposed, it must be removed from any point of influence, and if a person is known to be the point of origin, that person must be removed from the church. Any attempt to reestablish this person will result in the same future dilemmas and a relapse of the infection. If this spirit is given permission to stay, or if it is not handled strictly and immediately, it will cause problems for years to come, and whoever was the influencer will continue to infect all those who are around him or her. It is imperative to know that this spirit is never to be taken lightly. The Amalekites were related to the Edomites, so any form of compromise will only entice it more!

The Bible paints a very clear picture of the errors the Israelites stumbled into while dealing with the Amalekites, but it also gives a very precise way to victory as well. The most well-known story of achievement is where the Amalekites were the defeated recipients of the fight where Moses's hands were held up by Hur and his brother Aaron. As long as Moses's arms were supported and remained high in the air, the Israelites tasted victory, but the minute his arms would drop, Israel would start to feel the weight of defeat. This is the exact spiritual key to victory over this oppressive spirit! The apostle, or lead pastor of the church, or church leadership in general, cannot stand against this spirit alone. They will grow weary and faint no matter how strong they start this race out. This is a team effort, and success can only be achieved by rallying around leadership and giving them the much-needed support and assistance, they need. The only way to overcome this disgusting Amalekite spirit is to come together in support and unity under leadership, and to stop any and all complaining, regardless of whether it is felt to be just.

Now, arms in the Bible always represent influence, power, and means of support and conquest. This is why as the Amalekite spirit increases in its influence, church growth, evangelism, and community impact plummet. In short, the reach of the church is shortened. Leadership must delegate responsibility to those equipped to carry it and put an immediate end to any grumbling or complaining in the church. In the physical, this is done in the same way Moses was instructed by his father-in-law, Jethro, to select judges to help govern the people. This means other church leadership must be put into place. In the spirit, the way that Moses allowed Aaron and Hur to hold up his arms, the church must lift up and support the heads of the church by prayer and fasting, and with their ever-increasing workload. Could you imagine where Israel would have been if Moses had told Jethro that he could handle everything by himself, or if Moses hadn't allowed his assistants to grab on and give his arms a rest? It takes a stronger leader to recognize gifts, delegate responsibilities, and trust his people than it does to run the show alone. Do not be so prideful or fall victim to having a lack of trust in whom God has brought you that you refuse, ignore, or overlook the Aarons and Hurs who will help accomplish the victory. This will spread out the weight of responsibility and defuse the protesting and moaning. These are all open doors that the Amalekite spirit looks for in order to influence the start of constant bleating of a church's sheep. And keep in mind that one sheep never cries out alone!

When Paul said that one gift is not better than another, he was talking about the gifts of people given to the church. The arm can't say to the leg, "I don't need you." The eye can't say to the nose, "I'm better than you are." We all need each other! This is the only way to find, expose, and overcome this cleverly infiltrating spirit. United we stand, but divided we fall victim to the influence of the Amalakites!

Leaders: Write the vision and make it plain. Cast it out and make it tangible so that the people have the opportunity to grab hold and climb on board with it. And for those people who grab hold of the vision, give them the opportunity to use their God-given spiritual gifts to help flourish it.

Church members and other church leadership: Take every effort to understand and support the vision of the church. Be like David and never set your hand against God's anointed by talking against the heads of the church. Our words have power, and the Amalekite spirit loves to use negative words to empower division. If there's a mistake made, make every attempt to help rectify it. For if God restores everything, and the church is designed to be His image and heart in this world, then it too should forgive and restore as well! Man is made in the image of the Almighty Himself, and any words spoken against that image is indirectly spoken against God. When people talk negatively about the church in any manner and for any reason, they are being dismissive and inadvertently destructive to the very thing Jesus died to make spotless and blameless. We cannot forget that the church is just people, going through a process just like everyone else, and that mistakes will be made. The only question that needs to be asked is, "How will the mistakes be recovered and worked together for the good and advancement of the church and to bring God glory, so that Jesus Christ can receive the full reward of His suffering?"

Chapter 10

Final Thoughts

Watch yourself so that you make no covenant with
the inhabitants of the land where you are going,
lest it become a snare in your midst. (Exodus
34:12)

Walking the Fence

This was not just the command that God set forth for Israel before
they inherited their Promised Land. This was also the biggest
stumbling block they repeatedly tripped over. The Israelites
continually ignored Yahweh's warning that if they made a
covenant with any of their enemies, or if they tried to rectify and
allow their foes to live among them in any way, they would fall
into ongoing and persistent snares and pitfalls. Remembering
that Israel was walking out physically what Christians walk out
spiritually today, this is one of the greatest temptations for the
sons and daughters of God on this side of the New Testament as
well. The idea of dabbling in the world's system of things, playing
with sin, or trying a small taste of what society says is good is
when believers unknowingly or knowingly make covenants and
open doors to the enemies that only wish to steal, kill, and destroy

their destines. Some opened doors take years to realize they were opened, and some are noticed immediately.

Israel never thought it was bad to take plunder for themselves, to keep women and children alive, or to incorporate a certain idol into their everyday worship of Yahweh. They felt that as long as Elohim was placed first, everything was okay and they were able to do whatever they wanted. Christians today think along the same lines and allow their minds to ponder and get caught up on the thoughts of things: "It's okay to be around certain things and certain people as long as it's rectified with the idea that the goal is to eventually preach the gospel. It's fine to take something seemingly harmless, like a tithe or stolen property, as long as the church is doing well financially, or if I'm not the ones actually doing the stealing." The problem is that certain things don't just open doors but also put us in agreement with the enemy and give him legal right to cause havoc in our lives, whether or not we're aware of it. There are tons of examples that can be set forth that would probably take up an extensive number of books, and eventually one of those examples would hit home and bring conviction, but the focus boils all those decisions down to whether it's right, or wrong, and whether it's either out of love or selfishness.

Christians are called to be the light of the world and to reflect the love of a perfect heavenly Father, and that can't be done while dabbling in sin and playing with the devil's toys. God says if you're lukewarm, He will spit you out! That's not only because He knows the importance of setting forth a good example that can't bring on reproach, but it's also because the love of the Father yearns to see His children live out a life in the fullness of His design. God knows that if Christians have one foot in the world and one foot in the kingdom, they will deny themselves the fullness of both lifestyles. If you're playing the fence and caught in the middle, you'll be denying yourself what the world has to offer, and you're closing off the opportunity to walk into the fullness of what God has to offer. The Holy Spirit is *always* speaking to people. He is the only One content with who you are, right where you are, right when you are. However, it's His role to convict you of sin and of righteousness and, by doing so, lead you into a transformational encounter that leaves you looking more and more like Jesus Christ. It's so important to know that even when you are not content, happy, and accepting of yourself, the Holy Spirit is so overjoyed and deeply in love with you right where you're at. When you do something right and in alignment with the kingdom, His convictions of righteousness give you a pat on the back of approval and of joy. When you do something opposite of the standard that Jesus modeled and slip into that gray area, His convictions of sin remind you of who you are in Christ—which is that you are still righteous and holy not by your works, but by the work that Jesus did on the cross—and that you're still working things out which is why you stumbled and fell in the first place and how to correct the error. This is a process, and everyone will continue to work salvation out with fear and trembling. But when Christians dip a toe into the world's play box to see how far they can get without any backlash, or when they just jump in completely, they numb the voice of the Holy Spirit convicting them of where and how they are falling short. For believers, falling short is a painful reminder of how they are missing Christ's glorious standard. Therefore, the easiest thing to do is ignore this prompting of conviction in order to remain playing in the box. This sneaky trick of the enemy leads Christians into habitually ignoring the voice of the Holy Spirit, which in turn leaves their hearts voluntarily separated from God's discipline and His loving approval. This was what Adam and Eve did in the garden when they hid from God. Elohim still desired fellowship and relationship with them, but it was their knowledge of the evil they'd committed that led them to hide themselves from His presence. When Christians become lukewarm, they hide themselves from the very One who cares the most about them. When a sheep can't hear the voice of its Shepherd, it feels lost, alone, and helpless—and worse yet, it leaves itself vulnerable to the attacks of the wolves. Walking the fence and dabbling in sin has much deeper consequences than many believers understand!

Where's Your Focus?

The fight against Satan and his angels comes in many different forms, but his bag of tricks always remains the same. Whether it's a spiritual battle or is mental, emotional, or physical, Lucifer will try his hand from any angle and as many times as it takes until something works. He is relentless and extremely patient and will play any hand he's dealt, but keep in mind his biggest trick is to call a bluff and hope you fold. He was, and still is, the craftiest of all the animals, so it would be a huge error to not acknowledge the fact that if left unchecked, he's dangerous.

However, there's no need to focus on him and give fear the opportunity to take root in your heart. There's a difference between acknowledging and focusing. The Bible tells us to give no place to fear, and it reminds us that although the devil may prowl around like a roaring lion, seeking someone to devour, he is and was no match for the Spirit that raised the Savior from a burrowed tomb. Keep in mind that same Spirit is now living in every single Christian! When the reality of how big God is becomes a natural part of your thinking, it is impossible to make the devil small enough. He becomes so insignificant in comparison to the revelation of who Jesus Christ is and what He's made everyone who believes to be, He removes all the fear the devil could try and shake up in you.

Israel had many enemies and faced extreme challenges that tested their faith and willpower to press forward. If the devil's motive never changes, what makes Christians today believe that this walk of salvation will be any different for them? In this life, you will face hardships, persecution, ridicule, mockery, false teachings, testing, and terrible situations and circumstances. The truth is we live in a world where we were graciously given a free will, and there's always the option to sin. Not every bad or evil thing that happens to you is an attack of the enemy; sometimes these things happen as a result of someone else's free will and because of the effect sin has on the world around us. Let it be a settled fact that under no circumstances is God the orchestrator of sickness and disease. The root always leads back to Satan and his crafty initiation of man into a life of sin. When believers focus on the devil and blame him for everything that goes wrong, all they're doing is giving him more power and influence and allowing fear to grow in the hearts of people around them. Remember that Satan started out in the book of Genesis as a serpent, but by the time we get to the book of Revelation, he's a dragon! Whatever you choose to focus on, whether it's good or bad, will grow.

As a result of their victories in the wilderness and the conquest of the Promised Land, and combined with the God they served, Israel never had to face some enemies. Enemies like the Girgashites, Perizzites, and Jebusites fled the land on their own, and eventually these nations were never heard about again. This is a sobering reminder that not only does God fight some battles for His children without their knowledge, but if you stick to the course Elohim has set before you, there are enemies you'll never have to face unless you're looking for them.

The Cause of Sickness and Disease

The human being was built by the Creator Himself to be a four-part being: spiritual, mental, physical, and emotional. Gender doesn't play a role; whether a person is male or female, he or she will function at 25 percent in each one of these categories. Therefore, it's crucial to make sure you're keeping up with all four of these areas. If one lags behind, the other three areas will have to attempt to make up for it. The sad reality is each of these areas is designed to function only at 25 percent, so if one area is lacking, it throws off the entire body, and the struggle to try to regulate yourself and feel "normal" kicks into overdrive. This results in sickness, diseases, exhaustion, depression, feeling separated from God, a lack of motivation, confusion, and more, but the worst outcome is that it leaves an open door and a prime opportunity for the enemy to influence you. Things like daily scriptural reading, devotion time, eating right, exercise, continued education, book reading, and being around a healthy community of friends and family are ways to keep all four of these areas in top functioning order and resilient against the pressures and schemes of the devil.

Now, being spirit first is different than being spiritual. Remember, spirit first only means that it was originally Yahweh's design for all people to be Spirit led. This revelation leads to many different answers regarding some of the most common questions people struggle with today. Understanding that human beings are structured to be spirit first allows you to shift your thinking enough to grasp the truth as to why, when people put themselves physically first, there's such a breakdown in things around us, especially in our bodies. It was stated previously in this chapter that God is not the orchestrator of sickness and disease, but rest assured He is the One who wants to heal it!

Most sicknesses and diseases, with the exception of just a few, have their start as a spiritual root. Because we are spirit-first beings, if there is a problem spiritually, it will *always* manifest physically. This is the exact reason Jesus took thirty-nine lashes to His body at the whipping post. There is no coincidence that science has narrowed down all sicknesses and diseases to an original thirty-nine strands. Every sickness and disease known to humankind can be brought back to these original thirty-nine starting points, and ten times out of ten, if there's a physical sickness or disease making its way to the surface of your body, there's a spiritual root as the cause of it. However, it is important to know that if there is an ailment in your body that was caused by an outside force, such as radiation that caused cancer, a car accident that caused lasting bodily injury, or anything else that was derived from a trauma or something out of your control, this is not a spiritual root. Therefore, because it's not an issue of the heart, it can and will usually result in an immediate miracle, or you will be able to see an obvious healing is taking place. This can be by immediate improvement in the affected area, or an immediate decrease in pain. Something will indicate that God is working and that you can stand upon the promise that what He started, He is faithful to complete!

Here is a list of the most common sicknesses and diseases, as well as the spiritual roots that have caused them. Keep in mind that once you recognize the root, this allows you the opportunity to fight against it! For example, if you find the root is unforgiveness, as you work through the process of forgiving, the sickness loses its hold. Some sicknesses and diseases miraculously disappear the second the root is dealt with accordingly; others take time, and it's a process of healing. God could heal in an instant everyone dealing from spiritually rooted sickness and disease, but if He doesn't deal with the spiritual issue, the sickness and disease can manifest again. This is why we see people relapse, or why we pray for some and don't see an immediate healing. It's impossible to pray and have nothing happen, so don't let a delayed answer discourage you from praying. Whether or not you see it happening, something is taking place, and when we target these spiritual roots, we tip the scales in our favor and give the suffering person the opportunity to step into a miracle. It's also important to know that there is no exact formula for anything involving the kingdom. God is simply God! He's the alpha and the omega, the beginning and the end, the all-knowing and all-loving. His thoughts are higher than our thoughts, and more than anything, His ways are tremendously better than our ways. As believers, we can rest assured that God is working everything in love because He is love, and He is working everything for the good because He is good. All we need to do is put our confidence in Him, not be ignorant to the devil's schemes, and position ourselves to receive the blessings He most desperately wants to pour out over us!

Spiritual Roots of Diseases

—❧— ————•≻●≺•———— —☙—

Accident Prone
Could be a spiritual rooted problem of low self-image or fear.

Adult on-set Diabetes
Rooted in self-rejection, self-bitterness and self-hatred. Usually from long-term rejection, abuse, or abandonment from a parent or guardian or spouse. The pancreas is being attacked by the white corpuscles that are supposed to guard us from disease. Yet because this individual has been attacking for years with guilt and self-hatred, the body begins to attack as well.

Acoustic Neuroma
This is a rare tumor and is hereditary, with a gene missing in that person. Rooted in high-stress situations and fear.

Allergies
All allergies are rooted in fear, anxiety, and stress. A compromised (broken) immune system. Something happened to cause this person to be broken to the point of almost no return. Took a long time to get over: "A merry heart does good like a medicine, but a broken spirit dries up the bones" Allergies are connected with the bone marrow being dried up! It's medically proven. It is not because a person is reacting to a chemical or smell. It doesn't show up on a RAS test. There's a compromised immune system here.

Some people believe it's because they have been exposed to too many chemicals. That is a lie! What broke the system are long-term fear, anxiety, and stress. When you have a compromised immune system, you'll have allergies. Long-term fear, anxiety, and stress will destroy your immune system. When you have a breakdown in this area, you may be allergic to more than one thing; this is a phobic disease, and panic attacks are associated with it. Deut 28:65–68 states anxiety comes to one who does not fear the Lord. Separation between us and God is the sin of unforgiveness.

Attention Deficit Disorder (ADD)
Serotonin deficiency: self-hatred, self-bitterness. The reversal would be to get the individual to love themselves.

Alzheimer's
White corpuscle deviate behavior. This is a problem with the self.

Angina
Rooted in fear and anxiety.

Anorexia
Rooted in self-hatred, self-rejection, self-bitterness, insecurity, and lack of self-esteem. The serotonin levels are lowered, caused by not feeling good about yourself. If you felt good about yourself, your serotonin levels would be normal, and you would not have these diseases. This person becomes driven in everything and having to perform to be accepted.

Bulimia
It could be genetic as well, but the root is still spiritual from that ancestor. Also, it can be from a spirit of "control", matriarchal, witchcraft, etc. This is also known as a self-mutilation. Anytime there is cell mutation, it is a result of bitterness. This is a hidden

addiction to food. The individual has a desire to eat but won't because he or she has a fear he or she won't be able to stop.

Feelings of no value. They feel rejected and unloved. This could also be rejecting and not loving toward themselves.

Need to identify the person(s) involved in this and begin the healing through confession and forgiveness.

Aneurysms

Aneurysms, strokes, and heart attacks are caused from exploding blood vessels, varicose veins, and hemorrhoids. They all have something in common: unresolved rage and anger.

Arthritis

See Rheumatoid Arthritis.

Asthma

Rooted in fear and anxiety. It wasn't what the person was breathing that caused the attack. There was something internally that was stiffening the cell walls. Cell wall rigidity. The toxins are building up in the person from the spiritual root. It only appears those "allergic" things are causing it, but that is the deception. We begin avoiding things, and now we have avoidance behavior on top of the real root! Fear is now even stronger because fear promotes avoidance.

Anti-unconogenital (Forms of Cancer)

Antigen also known as white blood cells.

God created in every cell two enzymes that are tied to your immune system; they are called anti-unconogens. If you have two in every cell, you will never get cancer. Two dimensions can destroy the cells: something internal and something external. Inherited cancer normally means that one anti-unconogen is present, and if that is destroyed, cancer can begin at any time. External destruction can be brought on by radiation, chemicals, or PCBs. Internal destruction is where the spiritual root needs to be dealt with, such as broken relationship of some kind, either with God, oneself, or with others. This too can destroy the anti-unconogens, resulting in cancer.

Autoimmune Disease
Diabetes, multiple sclerosis, rheumatoid arthritis, lupus, crone's disease, and other white corpuscle-deviate behavior. (The manifestations of self-hatred, self-guilt, self-conflict, self-rejection, self-bitterness, self-conflict, etc.) As the person attacks oneself spiritually, the body attacks the body physically, and the enemy joins in. When we attack ourselves with self-hate and bitterness, we are giving the white corpuscles permission to attack us as well, and we're giving the enemy permission to do the same!

Back Problems
Root can be in self-rejection. However, it has been noted that the occultism and false religions are usually associated with back problems.

Bladder Problems
Rooted in a compromised immune system.

Bone Problems
Psalm 31:10 states iniquity causes us to be weakened and our bones waste away. Sorrow in relationships with God, oneself, or others. Proverbs 3:6–8 says by acknowledging God in all our ways, but fearing the Lord (departing from evil), and by not taking your own advice but believing the Word of God, then it shall be health to thy navel and marrow to the bones. Disobedience to God's Word will cause your bones to dry up.

Bowel Problems (Cell wall Rigidity)

Causes the body to dry up the liquids that should soften the excretion, but it hardens instead and causes problems. Spiritual root is fear or being abandoned or rejected, resulting in self-rejection, self-bitterness, and self-hatred. Not accepting self due to a broken relationship with another. Other causes could be inherited curses. Nehemiah 2:9 states we are to break the curse on our lives and on our children's lives by confessing the sins of the fathers. Ezekiel 18:60–62 says it could be from jealousy of a husband who brings a curse on the wife, resulting in infidelity. Thoughts or intents of the heart need to be confessed. The problem can result in disease of bowel, intestines, thighs, barrenness, and a bloating stomach. Adultery can cause bowel problems too (Numbers 5:19). People have to seek the truth for their lives.

Breast Cancer

Can be inherited. Also from, exposure to radiation (mammograms). Breastfeeding of newborns helps prevent cancer (God's natural way of prevention)

Most breast cancer is a result of a spiritual problem. Ten percent of all breast cancer is caused by mammograms, which is a national statistic! Why? Because 10 percent of all women have a genetic code defect. Women should take a test before this test to be sure their unconogens are in each cell. We need two, and if there is only one, it will be destroyed by the X-ray, and it is guaranteed that individual will get breast cancer. If the two unconogens are present, you will never get breast cancer. (See Anti-unconogen for more details.) Deep-rooted bitterness and resentment, either with a mother or one or more sisters, results in breast cancer. We need to get right with our family members, especially if our husbands are not nurturing, because cancer attacks the nurturing part of the woman's body (breasts, etc.).

Cancer

Cancer cells develop in each of us all day long, but a peaceful heart and mind kills the cells! Peace of mind and with others and God is the antidote to cancers.

Results in outside or inside destruction. Outside could be from radiation, chemicals, PCBs, etc. Be aware of your surroundings: what you put in your mouth, household chemicals, and so forth. Inside results from a broken relationship with God, self, or others. Both destroy the anti-unconogens, and when two are not present in all cells, it results in cancer. So, what's going on inside of you? There's an old saying: "It eats at you like a cancer." When you meditate on hatred against an individual who has wronged you, as you start to focus on that with resentment, anger, hatred, retaliation, bitterness, and unforgiveness for a long period of time, your body is chemically manufacturing toxins out of bitterness and anger. These will create a volume of toxins and destroy anti-uncogenes; the cell is compromised, and you have cancer just like that! Helplessness breeds cancer.

Colon Cancer

Not sure right now the exact root, but unforgiveness is definitely part of it. We need to search our hearts and ask God whom we have not forgiven from our hearts!

Pancreas Cancer

Rooted in self-bitterness, self-rejection, self-hatred, and self-rejection. The white corpuscles attack the pancreas. Normally, this disease is diagnosed in early stages as diabetes, but long term it has a likelihood of developing into cancer.

Prostate Cancer

Self-conflict with being a man for prostate cancer. Self-rejection, self-hatred.

Throat Cancer
Broken spirit, unforgiveness, unresolved conflict with others and self, fear, and anxiety.

Uterine Cancer
See Ovarian Cancer

Candida
A peripheral disease along with yeast infections, fibromyalgia, catatonia, hypothyroidism, organic brain syndrome, retention of toxins, etc. They are not the problem; they are the manifestations of anxiety and fear brought on by being broken by a past relationship.

Cerebral Palsy
It's not a spiritual rooted disease. It's caused from a birth defect, such as no oxygen to the brain or a preemie baby. This will take a creative miracle from God.

Chronic Fatigue Syndrome (CFS)
Fear and anxiety brought on by a breakdown in relationship with parent or guardian, mostly of a father or male figure, resulting in the individual being exhausted all the time for no apparent reason. Driven to meet the expectations of a parent in order to receive love and acceptance. (See Parkinson's Disease; they have the same components.)

Colds/Flu
Viruses are not spiritually rooted. However, if the immune system is down, colds will take root. Spiritually rooted problem is in a broken immune system—self-doubt, guilt, and brokenness.

Compulsive Behavior
Rooted in serotonin deficiency. Self-problems.

Congestive Heart Failure
Rooted in fear and anxiety, bitterness, and self-rejection. "Men's heart's fail them for fear" (Luke 21:6). Lack of self-esteem.

Crohn's Disease
White corpuscle deviate behavior (autoimmune disease). Rooted in self-hatred, self-rejection, and guilt of not performing perfectly to gain love, affection, and acceptance of an unloving parent, or striving to earn the love of a parent.

Depression
Generic term. It is a result of chemical imbalance, and each person needs to have considerable investigation. Depression is caused from an unloving spirit toward self, resulting in self-rejection or rejection of another. Anytime you come into rejection of self, this will manifest in your body. "Hope deferred makes the heart sick" (Proverbs 13:2).

A loss of expectation in life, producing crushing of the human spirit.

Depression comes from anxiety.

Diabetes
White corpuscle deviate behavior (autoimmune disease). Self-rejection, self-hate, guilt, self-bitterness. However, it began with separation from another. The seed is rejection of a father. Father establishes the emotional welfare of a child. Fear of humans sets in. Hatred of humans sets in.

Diverticulitis
Rooted in rage and anger. Brought on by fear and anxiety.

Dizziness
Needs to be dealt with on an individual basis.

Eczema, Psoriasis
Rooted in fear and anxiety. See Psoriasis for more detail.

Elevated Cholesterol
Rooted in fear. Only certain people have a predisposition to hardening of the arteries. Triglycerides can be related to a certain inherited problem. The Bible says that all heart problems are related to fear. Rooted in paranoia and fear.

Electro Magnetic Field Syndrome (EMFS)
Electricity affects them adversely. Rooted in fear and anxiety. Same as MCS/EI.

Environment Illness (EI)
People who cannot tolerate smells, fumes, fabrics, etc.
    Rooted in fear and anxiety brought on by a breakdown in relationship with a parent or guardian, mostly of a father or male figure.

Emphysema
Usually the product of smoking. If it's a spiritually rooted disease or genetic, there is a cure. Once dealt with the spiritual aspect, if any, then pray for a miracle so the genetics will change and the problem won't reappear. And of course, stop smoking. (Smoking is from a spiritually rooted problem of addiction, a void that needs filling.)

Epilepsy
Unclean spirit (Mark 9:17).
    This is a result of an evil spirit, and it needs to be cast out. It's even documented in the Bible. Where it came from doesn't matter; it still needs to be dealt with as a spirit. If it comes through an illness or a knock on the head, it's an open door for the enemy to

come in with the disease. Injury can open the door to epilepsy. Grand mal seizures can be caused by an injury, however a spirit enters through that door of injury and needs to be cast out. Ask God to heal that individual after ministry.

Eye Problems
Unforgiving your enemies is a spiritual root. Grief here comes from broken relationship with others.

Fibromyalgia
Pain that is localized or all over the body, with no inflammation and no reason. Can come in by an injury, but most of the time it's a spiritual root. Psychogenic pain (thought). The hypothalamus secretes hormone into a nerve, but it causes the flesh to have pain because there is no place for this hormone to go, but it pulsates causing fibromyalgia. Rooted in fear and anxiety. Broken relationship with parent or guardian. Emotional roots of fibromyalgia: stress, tension, depression, anxiety, striving, fear, or depression. Physical manifestations: muscle pain, joint pain and tenderness, no swelling. Serotonin deficiency, resulting in hatred toward self. An emotional conflict. There is always a stressor. There is a reason!

Not having had the love needed to help them know how to love themselves.

Peace is the antidote!

Fibroid Cysts
Caused by self-hatred that was caused from bitterness of a mother. Can be connected with matriarchal control in the home.

Fear
This is a spirit. "For God has not given us the spirit of fear, but power, love and a sound mind." (2 Timothy 1:7) These same three things are also the "kingdom of God." "For the Kingdom of God is

not meat and drink, but righteousness, peace and joy in the Holy Ghost." (Romans 14:17) We need to recognize fear as a spirit, treat it as such, and begin to walk out those fearful situations. Genesis 3:10 indicates that fear comes by disobedience, which comes from the Spirit of Fear (enemy).

Fluid Retention
A new class of diseases is known as cell wall rigidity. The spiritual root behind this problem is fear, anxiety, and stress. This is also documented as a medical prognosis as well. This includes all diseases such as glaucoma, asthma, and other types of fluid retention diseases.

Gout
Rooted in extreme fear.

Gallbladder Stone
Caused by self-hatred and self-rejection. Can be someone who is overweight. Primarily a female disorder. Usually hits women who have had children or who may consider themselves overweight. Possibly related to self-hatred and self-rejection over being "fat," and avoiding all fat when that part of the body is designed to handle it.

Gastrointestinal Problems
All are rooted in fear and anxiety. Hiatal hernia, leaky gut, malabsorption (cell wall rigidity), constipation, and diarrhea.

Glaucoma
Fear and anxiety cause cell wall rigidity.

Hashimoto disease
A breakdown in relationship with God or others. Anxiety and fear.

Heart Problems (Hardening of Arteries)
Ezekiel 11:19 says, "I will replace your hardened heart with a heart of flesh—compassion, love, peace, gentleness, forgiveness."

Fear and anxiety, not cholesterol.

Keep your heart with all diligence (talking about adhering to wisdom), for out of it flows the issues of life. If you want life? Then be diligent in putting in your heart the things from God, removing out of the heart that which is not from God.

Heartburn (Mitral Valve Prolapse)
Caused by stress and anxiety. Rooted in fear.

Heart Murmur
Genetic disease. You have to get rid of the spiritual root and ask God to change the genetic code so it won't be passed on anymore. Rooted in fear and anxiety.

Heart Palpitations
Rooted in fear and anxiety.

Hernias
Inherited or occupational strain. The tear needs to be healed by God.

Hemorrhoids
Unresolved rage and anger.

High Blood Pressure
Unresolved rage and anger.

Hyperthyroidism
Very serious emotional conflict.

Hypertension
Long-term fear and anxiety.

Hypothyroidism
A breakdown in relationship with God, others, or self. Brings on fear and anxiety. Can be a self-conflict problem, unloving spirit toward self.

Hives
Rooted in fear and anxiety.

Hodgkin's Disease
Deep-rooted bitterness, resentment, and self-hatred coming from rejection (in most cases by a father).

Irritable Bowel Syndrome
Root is in fear and anxiety. Need to find out where the conflict is and deal with it.

Insanity
Dumb and deaf spirit that needs to be cast out! (Any problems from the neck up is a result of a deaf and dumb spirit.) Jesus cast out spirits of those who were insane.

Insomnia
Unresolved conflict.

Irregular Heartbeat
Can be inherited, and if it has been inherited you have inherited the spirit of fear. Fear and anxiety cause rhythmic problems, even if it is genetic.

Lack of Self-esteem

Chronic depression can be caused by suppressed anger. Crying is a natural cleanser. Confess your sins (faults) so that you may be healed (James 5:16). You need time to become trusting and vulnerable again.

Leukemia

There are twenty-three kinds of leukemia. Each one could have a differing root. Spiritual root may be deep-rooted bitterness, resentment, and self-hatred coming from rejection (by a father in most cases).

Lower Back Pain

Range of things: sciatica, degenerative disc, slip disc, osteoarthritis, spondylosis, scoliosis.

It can be inherited, and it's probably some kind of conflict with a female (usually the mother). Any arthritis in the back is rooted in bitterness against yourself, or any unresolved issue. Accidents that cause back problems need to be healed by God.

Spiritual root: self-rejection, self-bitterness, self-conflict.

Lupus

White corpuscle deviate behavior (autoimmune disease). They attack the connective tissue of the organs and eat it. Self-hatred, guilt, and condemnation.

Manic Depression

A genetic inherited mental problem. Long-term manic depressants can become psychotic. People demonstrating this is very dangerous because they need professional attention and drugs until it can be dealt with spiritually.

Male victimization causes manic depression in women. Genetic code defect comes in, and spirit of infirmity comes in. Could be brought in by false religion, occult, witchcraft, satanic ritual abuse, Ouija boards, etc.

Multiple Chemical Sensitivity Disorder (MCSD)

It's a direct result of a breakup in a relationship between the person and someone else, usually a close family member, and it always includes one of the following circumstances: physical abuse, verbal abuse, sexual abuse, and a drive to meet the domineering, cold parent in order to receive love. This breaks the human spirit, allowing the entrance of fear. If we don't get the nurturing, it causes a breaking in mind and body connection. Long-term fear results in running from and avoiding that person or place, resulting in more fear and anxiety.

Rooted in fear and anxiety brought on by a breakdown in relationship with parent or guardian (usually a father or male figure).

In abuse, no one should stay in that situation. Because of this brokenness, this person can't give love without fear.

Multiple Sclerosis

White corpuscle deviate behavior (autoimmune disease). Self-hate, shame, self-bitterness, self-rejection, any self-conflict. *Sclerosis* is one being eaten, and *multiple* is that many are being eaten throughout the body.

You cannot simply lay hands on this person; there is a definite spiritual root that has to be dealt with, and then healing will follow.

Multiple Personality Disorder (MPD)

Evil spirits that need to be cast out. The door can be opened through satanic ritual abuse (SRA) or a trauma that allows the evil spirits to come in to help that person deal with the trauma.

Migraine

Internalized conflict. Mad at self for not handling situations or people the way one intended. Conflict with self over a person or situation.

Fear and anxiety. Conflict with self. Self-rejection, self-bitterness, self-hatred, and guilt caused by fear.

Osteoarthritis
Can be rooted in self-hatred and rejection.

Osteoporosis
Bitterness, envy, and jealousy. Controlling nature. Comes from an evil root of matriarchal leadership in the home.

Ovarian Cancer
Caused by promiscuity or hatred at being female. Not accepting yourself as a woman.

Obsessive Compulsive Behavior (OCD)
Rejection and self-rejection

Ovarian Cysts
Always a result from a conflict with the mother, without exception. (Same as breast cysts.)

Paranoia
Mirrors manic depression. Permanent lowered serotonin levels. Self-problem.

Parkinson's Disease
Lost hope someplace. They never amounted to what was expected of them, from others or from themselves. They became driven to please others but were never quite accepted. They were rejected and broken in spirit. Their hearts became sick, and they began living in hopelessness, which led to self-hatred, self-bitterness, self-guilt, and conflict with the self.

Driven, failure, don't measure up, never meet own or other's expectations, or never had expectations fulfilled.

Pinched Nerve
Not a spiritual problem. We need to ask God to release that nerve.

Psoriasis
Fear and anxiety coupled with self-hatred and rejection. They struggle with their own identity, and the body responds.

Ringing in Ears
Damage from accident or loud noise. This opens the door to a spirit. Witchcraft and occult open the door as well. A spirit has to be cast out. Repent from sins and receive healing from God.

Rashes
Rooted in fear, anxiety, and stress.

Rheumatoid Arthritis
Rooted in bitterness and unforgiveness toward another, dead or alive, resulting in self-rejection, self-hate, and guilt.

Seizures (Various Types)
Seizures need to be looked at one case at a time. We need to deal with casting out the deaf and dumb spirit in any seizure case. (See Epilepsy for more information.)

Sciatica
Inflammation, usually left sided; most of the time it's considered a spirit. (See Back Problems). Roots of self-hatred and self-bitterness.

Sinusitis
Rooted in fear and anxiety.

Sleep Apnea/Sleep Disorders
All sleep disorders are caused by neurological interference or by hormone over secretion resulting from unresolved conflict.

With regard to sleep apnea, it would have its root in a deaf and dumb spirit. Someone who has great depression, great occultism, false religion, or somewhere along the way has opened the door.

Schizophrenia
Involves over secretion of serotonin and epinephrine. Caused by conflict within relating to a confused relationship with family members; normally it's a parent that says one thing and does another, but wanting the child to do what is right even though the parent does the exact opposite. This causes confusion in a child's mind. The child begins to question oneself, resulting in self-rejection, self-guilt, and bitterness.

Scoliosis
An evil spirit. Needs to be cast out. Then ask God for a creative miracle of the body.

Shingles
Anxiety and fear disorder.

Spondylosis/Osteoarthritis
Result of injury to possibly compromised tissue. The immune system is affected here. (See Back Problem.)

Strokes
Unresolved rage and anger; it can be inherited.

Sty
Anxiety defect.

Tuberculosis (TB)
It's a virus and isn't a spiritual problem. We need God to heal that through prayer.

Temporomandibular Joint (TMJ)
Rooted in fear and anxiety.

Ulcerative Colitis
Fear and anxiety defect. Cause is stress and unresolved conflict. (Could even be with oneself.)

Ulcers
Fear and anxiety open the door. Cause is anxiety and stress.

Varicose Veins
Unresolved rage and anger.

Vaginitis
See Candida.

Yeast Infections
See Candida

Final Thoughts

Obviously, there are many variations and avenues the devil and his minions can take to influence your mind and pull you away from being a spirit-first Christian. There is no "one size fits all," and for each person, the path to victory over the enemy looks different. However, if you apply what you've read in this book, the weapons to fighting that disgusting devil will always be the same. There are different approaches Satan will use to launch these attacks at you, but once the enemy is recognized, the tactic of defeating it will always remain the same.

Under Joshua, the Israelites controlled most of Canaan, but they did not obey God's command to eradicate the nations that stood against them, and as a result it would be the cause of their undoing for generations to come. This, seemingly small act of disobedience would lead to more problems with many other enemies. These previous chapters of enemies are the basic adversaries launched at the sons and daughters of God to this day. The devil has not changed his battle plans! There are countless enemies that can spring up as a result of not dealing with these foundational foes. Do not be like Israel and compromise God's commands by turning a blind eye to even the smallest hint of the enemy. A tiny bit of yeast will find its way through the entire batch of dough. All the devil needs is a small crack in the door to slide his foot in and have access to your entire house. Shut the door, bolt it, and don't open it no matter how sweet the temptation may sound from the other side. In such a time as this, there is too much at stake, and this war must be taken seriously. Your life and the lives of others depend on your obedience and willingness to stand apart and answer the call that's over your life with boldness and a determination to succeed! Simply put, you are spirit first—now walk in it!

Final Prayer

My gracious heavenly Father,

I pray that You seal up every word in this book in the hearts of those who read them. Let them be played back across their mind throughout the day and while they sleep. Let each piece of Your wisdom found within these pages grow them deeper in the understanding of who You are and who You're making them to be. Expand their minds to be able to grasp what they have read. I bless them all to take it further and deeper than You have allowed me to go. I pray that You will let my greatest revelation be their starting block. Let my ceiling be their floor! Expand their territory and prosper their land. May this book impact many and be used for the glory and expansion of Your kingdom. All for the glory and honor of my most precious friend and brother, my Savior, Jesus Christ. For His glory forever. Amen.

Salvation

I would not feel right ending this book without extending the opportunity for those who do not know Jesus, or who want to start the process over again, to accept Him as their Savior.

Accepting Jesus doesn't mean you have it all together or have all the answers. In fact, accepting Him means you don't have the answers, but you want to work towards them. Jesus did something we could never do: give us free access to the presence of God. Accepting Him as your Savior is simply the initial handshake into a relationship where you get to ask questions, make mistakes, walk into victories, and feel loved and accepted. Life is a journey filled with ups and downs, but it assures you that you'll never be alone. Walking with God is a lifelong process, but allowing Jesus to be your Savior and granting the Holy Spirit the role of your guide is just the first step.

There isn't some secret prayer or magical words. It's about acknowledging that we all make mistakes and then telling Jesus that you believe in Him and what He did on the cross in order to take away the punishment of those mistakes. This is how you acknowledge that you want to start a relationship with Him. There's only one way to God, and that's by accepting His Son, Jesus, as Savior. It's not something you say with your mouth; it's something you do in your heart. The Bible says we accept Jesus in our hearts and then confess Him with our mouths by talking about the salvation we walked into and the good things He does in our lives. Jesus lived the sinless life we couldn't so that when we receive Him as Savior, we receive His perfection too. Does that mean we walk out the rest of our lives perfectly? Of course not! But it does mean we're seen as perfect in our heavenly Father's eyes no matter what! That's exactly what Jesus died for.

If you have never accepted Jesus, open your heart and let Him in. Begin to ask Him questions and build a relationship. In time, it will grow, things will get easier, and His voice will get clearer and louder. Just give it time!

If you have accepted Jesus as Savior before, but you've wandered off in some areas, stop for a moment and reset. God still loves you, and He's been waiting for you to come back home. He holds no record of your wrongs, and all He truly cares about is loving you. He's doesn't want to punish you or make you pay for the things you did wrong while wandering around. He wants to restore your relationship and throw a party for His child's return.

If you've been compromising in some areas, stop and reset. You are a powerful person! Ask yourself, "What void am I filling with the compromise I've been settling for?" Stop doing it, get help if you need to, get accountability partners if you can, and let God be the filler of that void. That is the desire of His heart: to fill every empty place, and to take over all the places filled with toxic waste. You haven't thrown away your purpose or your inheritance. All you have to do is start walking in it again!

The end of this book signifies a fresh start for everyone reading it. Take a deep breath and enjoy it! God breathes out so you can breathe in! You're blessed!

Printed in the United States
By Bookmasters